Shastra Wisdom

English, Volume 1

The History of Hinduism

Embracing Timeless Traditions, Inspiring Modern Living

HEMAL SHAH

Shastra Wisdom – History of Hinduism
English, Vol 1.

FIRST EDITION, 2025.

Author: Hemal S. Shah

Publishing Country: Canada.

ISBN: 9781069377548

त्वमेव माता च पिता त्वमेव ।

त्वमेव बन्धुश्च सखा त्वमेव ।

त्वमेव विद्या द्रविणम् त्वमेव ।

त्वमेव सर्वम् मम देव देव ॥

Dedicated to my beloved ones who inspired me

in my journey

Contents

Introduction 7

About the Author 10

Disclaimer 11

1. HISTORY OF HINDUISM 15

  1.1.   What is Hinduism?....................................15

  1.2.   Origins of Hinduism 16

  1.3.   Practices and Beliefs 17

  1.4.   The Historical Timeline 23

    1.4.1.   Pre-Vedic Period 24

    1.4.2.   Vedic Period.................................26

    1.4.3.   Epic, Puranic, and Classical Age.............33

    1.4.4.   Medieval Period 37

    1.4.5.   Pre-modern Period 51

    1.4.6.   British Period 53

    1.4.7.   Modern Period 57

  1.5.   Hinduism, Buddhism & Jainism 59

  1.6.   Hinduism Denominations........................61

  1.7.   Hinduism Caste System 71

  1.8.   Hinduism Beliefs....................................79

    1.8.1.   Concept of Universal Soul (परमात्मा) 79

    1.8.2.   Concept of Atman (आत्मा) 80

    1.8.3.   Concept of Samsara.......................82

    1.8.4.   The Scriptures (धर्मग्रंथ)....................85

    1.8.5.   Concept of Cyclical Time (चक्रीय समय)...................86

    1.8.6.   Concept of Dharma (धर्म) 94

1.8.7.   Concept of Karma (कर्म) 97

2. APPENDIXES 104

2.1. Table of Figures 104

2.2. English Glossary 106

Introduction

Namaste and Welcome to Shastra Wisdom!

Shastra Wisdom is your gateway to exploring the timeless wisdom and vibrant traditions of Hinduism.

Shastra Wisdom is a platform dedicated to exploring Hinduism's rich heritage, spiritual teachings, and cultural vibrancy. From learning about yoga, meditation, philosophy, and rituals, to deepening your understanding of life's purpose, you will find guidance rooted in compassion and universal truths.

Hinduism, one of the world's oldest and most profound spiritual traditions, encourages us to embark on self-discovery, unity, and inner peace. Rooted in millennia of wisdom, Hinduism is not just a religion, but a way of life — a guide to understanding the complex relationship between ourselves, the universe, and the divine.

At the heart of Hinduism lies a deep reverence for diversity and harmony. Its teachings celebrate multiple paths to spiritual fulfillment, recognizing that everyone's journey is unique. From the sacred texts like the Vedas, Upanishads, and Bhagavad Gita, to the timeless wisdom of saints and sages, Hinduism offers a vast treasure of knowledge that has inspired countless generations.

Hinduism teaches us that divinity exists within each of us, in every being, and in every corner of the cosmos. The belief in karma, dharma, and the cycle of birth and rebirth urges us to live a life of integrity, purpose, and service. Through this platform, we aim to foster understanding, spiritual growth, and respect for the timeless values that Hinduism upholds.

Hinduism is one of the world's oldest and most complex religious traditions, evolving over millennia through a rich tapestry of philosophy, rituals, scriptures, and diverse cultural influences. This book takes you on a historical journey through Hinduism's origins, development, and transformation—from its early Vedic roots to its contemporary global presence.

Drawing from ancient texts, archaeological discoveries, and scholarly research, this work explores key milestones, influential thinkers, and the social, political, and spiritual forces that have shaped Hindu thought and practice. It delves into the rise of major philosophical schools, the impact of historical invasions and reform movements, and the continued relevance of Hinduism in the modern world.

With carefully curated content, visuals, and resources, I aim to foster understanding and appreciation of one of the world's oldest and most profound religions.

Whether you are a scholar, a seeker, or simply curious about the history of one of humanity's most enduring traditions, this book offers an engaging and insightful exploration of Hinduism's evolution and its profound influence on civilization.

Hinduism is not merely a religion but a living, evolving tradition that has touched countless lives over thousands of years. Its vast and intricate philosophies, rituals, and cultural practices form a mosaic that is as diverse as it is profound. Yet, in the modern world, Hinduism often remains misunderstood, reduced to stereotypes or confined to surface-level interpretations.

This book is my humble attempt to bridge the gap between the depth of Hinduism's teachings and its accessibility to a global audience. Drawing upon sacred texts, oral traditions, historical insights, and contemporary relevance, I have sought to present a comprehensive and balanced perspective on this ancient tradition.

This book is not an exhaustive compendium but rather a doorway to Hinduism's vast universe. It is designed to welcome readers of all backgrounds, whether they are deeply familiar with Hinduism or encountering it for the first time. I intend to explore its wisdom in a manner that resonates with both the intellect and the heart, offering insights that are timeless yet applicable to modern challenges.

I have approached this work with great respect and humility, aware of the immense responsibility that comes with writing about such a profound and complex tradition. Any shortcomings in capturing its depth are my own, and I invite readers to engage with this book not as the final word but as a starting point for further exploration.

I hope that this book inspires curiosity, understanding, and a deeper connection to the values that unite us as human beings. May it serve as a guide for those seeking knowledge, a companion for those on their spiritual journey, and a testament to the enduring legacy of Hinduism in our shared human story.

Let us walk together on this spiritual journey; learning, growing, and embracing the eternal truth: that we are all one, connected by the divine force that transcends time and space.

With gratitude,

HEMAL SHAH

About the Author

As the author of Shastra Wisdom, my goal is to create an inclusive and insightful space that explores the rich traditions, philosophies, and practices of Hinduism. This book aims to educate, inspire, and connect individuals from all backgrounds, offering an authentic understanding of Hinduism's historical significance and modern relevance.

Hinduism, one of the world's oldest spiritual traditions, provides profound wisdom on spirituality, ethics, and harmonious living. Through my journey as a student of Hinduism, I have engaged in continuous learning—hosting a podcast on Hinduism, and conversing with thought leaders, practitioners, and seekers, all of which have deepened my appreciation of Hindu values like dharma (righteous living), ahinsa (non-violence), and moksha (liberation).

Beyond education, my mission is to foster a community of dialogue, mutual respect, and cultural awareness. By promoting Hinduism's enduring values—compassion, self-realization, and unity—I hope to inspire spiritual growth and a deeper appreciation of this timeless tradition.

Whether you are a seeker, scholar, or simply curious, I invite you to join this journey of discovery. Together, we can celebrate and preserve Hindu wisdom for generations. For discussions or collaborations, connect with me at *shastrawisdom@gmail.com*.

HEMAL SHAH
ONTARIO. CANADA.

Disclaimer

This book is an exploration of Hinduism and its scriptures, written with the utmost respect and a sincere desire to share knowledge and insights about this ancient tradition. The interpretations, perspectives, and commentary presented here reflect the author's understanding and are not intended to represent the definitive views of any specific sect, organization, or individual.

Hinduism is a diverse and deeply personal faith with countless interpretations and practices. While every effort has been made to ensure accuracy, readers are encouraged to approach the content with an open mind and seek further study or consultation with learned scholars or practitioners for a more comprehensive understanding.

This book does not seek to promote or denigrate any religion, belief system, or cultural practice. It is intended for educational and informational purposes only. The author and publisher do not claim authority over religious doctrines and encourage readers to respect the beliefs and traditions of all communities.

Additionally, some content in this book, including images and rephrased text, may have been created or refined using AI tools. While AI has been utilized to enhance the presentation and accessibility of the material, the ideas and interpretations remain guided by human insight and effort. Readers are advised to consider the context of their own religious and cultural understanding when engaging with the material presented in this book.

Thank you.

Author

HEMAL SHAH

History of Hinduism

1. HISTORY OF HINDUISM

1.1. What is Hinduism?

Hinduism, also known as **Sanatan Dharma** or "The Eternal Way," is more than just a religion—it's a way of life that has existed for over 4,000+ years, making it one of the world's oldest traditions. Unlike many religions, Hinduism has no single founder or central authority, which allows for a wide range of beliefs and practices.

Hinduism embraces different paths to spirituality, including:

- Bhakti (Devotion) – Worshiping and loving the divine.

- Jnana (Knowledge) – Seeking wisdom and understanding.

- Dhyana (Meditation) – Focusing the mind for inner peace.

- Karma (Selfless Action) – Doing good without expecting rewards.

Despite its deep history and diversity, Hinduism is often misunderstood. Many misconceptions arise because people see only parts of it without understanding the bigger picture. Some aspects of Hindu culture and traditions have also been commercialized or misrepresented, sometimes for profit or political purposes, which distorts their true meaning.

To truly understand Hinduism, one must explore its philosophy, traditions, and spiritual teachings with an open mind. It has made profound contributions to philosophy, science, art, and culture over thousands of years. At its core, Hinduism teaches us to seek truth, live ethically, and find harmony with the universe.

Hinduism is a vast, intricate, and deeply personal blend of philosophy, spirituality, and culture. It teaches us to seek truth, live ethically, and strive for harmony with the universe.

1.2. Origins of Hinduism

> Note: Brahman (Sanskrit: ब्रह्मन्; IAST: Brahman) connotes the highest universal principle, the Ultimate Reality of the universe.

Hinduism is the oldest Living Region on Earth. The origins of Hinduism can be traced to the Indus Valley civilization in the Indian subcontinent, where its early followers lived. As one of the oldest religions in the world, evidence of Hinduism dates back around 5,000 years. By 1500 BCE[1], Hinduism had already developed as a rich philosophical and religious tradition that persists to this day. Without a single founder, pinpointing its precise beginnings is challenging, especially since Hinduism is distinctive not as a singular religion but as a collection of diverse traditions and philosophies. The term "Hinduism," was coined by British writers in the early 19th century, yet it refers to a vast cumulation of texts and practices, some dating as far back as the 2nd millennium BCE or earlier. If, as some scholars suggest, the Indus Valley civilization (3rd–2nd millennium BCE) is the source of these traditions, then Hinduism is the oldest living religion in the world. [2]".

A more precise and commonly used term to describe this belief system is Sanatan Dharma or Hindu Dharma. "Sanatan" means eternal, universal, and unchanging, while "Dharma" refers to harmony, compassion, truth, or natural law. Sanatan Dharma represents an eternal path, without beginning or end, prioritizing spiritual experience over religious and cultural practices. The term "Hindu" is believed to have originated from the name of the Sindhu River, a Sanskrit word used by the region's inhabitants. Other groups adopted the name for the land and its people in their languages.

While defining Hinduism can be complex, its origins lie in India. Most Hindus revere a core body of sacred texts known as the *Vedas* and

---

[1] Origins of Hinduism | Supplemental Resource | https://www.edu.gov.mb.ca/
[2] Hindu Association of the Northern Territory. https://tfhc.nt.gov.au/ & http://www.hinducouncil.com.au/

follow a shared system of values called *Dharma*. Hinduism has both monotheistic (one God) as well as polytheistic (many Gods) elements. Due to Hinduism's ancient roots and inclusive nature, which embraces a variety of beliefs and expressions, a broad range of philosophical doctrines have emerged over time. This diversity has led to the creation of additional sacred texts, such as the Upanishads, Puranas, Ramayana, and Bhagavad Gita, among others.

1.3. Practices and Beliefs

Figure 1 - Symbols used in Hinduism

Hinduism encompasses many practices and beliefs, making it difficult to define singularly. Jainism, Buddhism, and Sikhism, the three other major Indian religions, have their origins in Hinduism and share historical and conceptual ties. Unlike many different religions, Hinduism cannot be traced to a single founder, a single scripture, or a universally agreed-upon set of teachings. Over its long history, numerous influential figures with diverse teachings and philosophies have contributed to its development, producing many holy texts.

Hinduism is often considered more of a 'way of life' or a 'family of religions'[3] rather than a single religion, due to its incorporation of a wide range of religious ideas. , regarded as divine in origin, are considered direct transmissions of God's word, rather than being conveyed through a prophet.

---

[3] Hinduism. History. https://www.history.com/topics/religion/hinduism/

Hindu beliefs, codes of conduct, and social practices are derived from a broad collection of philosophical literature and scriptures, including the Vedas, the Upanishads, the Brahma Sutras, the Bhagavad Gita, and the epics Ramayana and Mahabharata—the latter being roughly six times the length of the Bible. Generally, one is recognized as a Hindu by being born into a Hindu family and practicing the faith, or by declaring oneself a Hindu. There is no formal process for conversion to or excommunication from Hinduism.

This rich tapestry of beliefs and practices reflects the profound complexity and depth of Hinduism. Among its many traditions, rituals are a vital component, ranging from daily worship (puja) conducted in homes and temples to grand festivals like Diwali, celebrating the victory of light over darkness, and Holi, the festival of colours symbolizing the arrival of spring and the victory of good over evil.

Moreover, yoga, in its various forms, including Bhakti (devotion), Jnana (knowledge), Karma (action), and Raja (meditation), is an integral practice aimed at achieving spiritual growth and self-realization. Yoga's diverse paths cater to different temperaments and life stages, contributing to the individual's spiritual journey.

Diverse as it is, Hinduism shares a common goal: the realization of the divine nature within and the attainment of moksha, or liberation from the cycle of birth and rebirth. The multiplicity of deities, philosophies, and rituals within Hinduism underscores its inclusive nature, allowing for a wide array of spiritual expressions and practices.

Hindus view the entire universe as God's creation and everything within it as an expression of God. They believe that each person is inherently divine, and the purpose of life is to seek and realize divinity within all of us.

Key Beliefs in Hinduism

Sanatan Dharma (Eternal Law) embodies a set of universal ethical and moral principles that guide a virtuous and truthful way of living. The Hindu ethical framework emphasizes values like truth, righteousness, love, peace, and non-violence. It posits that our beliefs shape our thoughts and attitudes, which in turn direct our actions, ultimately shaping our destiny. All Hindu ceremonies, rituals, and acts of worship conclude with a prayer for universal peace and harmony. The rituals are not merely acts of devotion but are deeply symbolic, representing profound philosophical concepts and life's transitions. For instance, the sacred thread ceremony marks a young person's entry into adulthood and their responsibilities towards society and spirituality. The Hindu wedding is another elaborate ceremony rich with symbolism, signifying the union of not only two individuals but their families and communities.

Hindu temples, often architectural marvels, are focal points for religious and social life, providing a space for worship, learning, and community gatherings. These temples house various deities, each representing different aspects of the supreme reality, and devotees may choose to worship one or many according to their personal inclinations and life circumstances.

Understanding the diversity within Hinduism requires recognizing that its practices and beliefs are context-dependent, varying across different regions, communities, and historical periods. This adaptability has allowed Hinduism to thrive and evolve over millennia, embracing change while maintaining core principles.

A central concept in Hindu philosophy is the law of karma—the principle of cause and effect, where every action generates a reaction that will be experienced in this life or the next. Life is viewed as a continuous process, with the essential life energy never being destroyed. Death is seen not as the end of life, but as part of the life process.

Consequently, Hindus believe in samsara, the cycle of birth, death, and rebirth, which continues until the individual soul, through self-realization of its inherent divinity, merges with the Absolute and achieves moksha, or liberation from the cycle of rebirth. Hindus believe that self-realization is attainable within one's lifetime, and thus it is considered the ultimate goal and destiny of all life. Despite lacking a distinct historical origin, single founder, central religious institution, or sole authoritative scripture, most traditions, sects, or schools within Hinduism share foundational concepts. Two of the most prominent are the oneness of existence and pluralism.

Over the centuries, various schools of thought developed within Hinduism through a dynamic of philosophical inquiry and debate. These schools, or *Darshanas*, emerged from timeless and universal questions, such as the purpose of life and the relationship between humans and the Divine (existence, pure being, light of consciousness). The term *darshana* means "seeing" and refers to different ways of perceiving the Divine and attaining *moksha* - liberation from the cycle of birth and rebirth.

7 Core Beliefs of Hinduism

- Belief 1. One Universal Soul
- Belief 2. Atman
- Belief 3. Samsara
- Belief 4. Vedas
- Belief 5. Cyclical Time
- Belief 6. Dharma
- Belief 7. Karma

One Universal Soul

Hindus view the entire universe as God's creation, and everything within it as an expression of God.

Atman

Atman refers to the soul. This philosophy teaches us that all living beings possess a soul, and each is a part of the supreme soul. In Hinduism, reincarnation is a core belief, that the soul is reborn after the body's death. The nature of each rebirth is shaped by one's karma which stems from the individual's actions from both current and previous lives

Samsara

Hindus believe in samsara, the cycle of birth, death, and rebirth, which continues until the individual soul, through self-realization of its inherent divinity, merges with the absolute being and achieves moksha, which is liberation from the rebirth cycle.

Vedas

Hindu beliefs, ethics, and social practices stem from numerous philosophical texts and scriptures, including the Vedas, Upanishads, Brahma Sutras, and Bhagavad Gita, as well as the epics Ramayana and Mahabharata.

Cyclical Time

The Hindu concept of time is cyclical, with the universe continuously transitioning through four distinct eras, called yugas. As time advances from one yuga to the next, human society experiences a gradual decline in moral, spiritual, and other qualities, becoming progressively more diminished.

Dharma

Dharma refers to the duties and responsibilities a Hindu should uphold in life. According to the Vedas, a well-rounded and meaningful life typically involves the balanced pursuit of right actions (dharma), material prosperity (artha), personal happiness (kama), and spiritual fulfillment. Dharma is often described as the law of righteousness, offering guidance to help individuals reach their highest potential.

Karma

Karma, a Sanskrit term meaning "action," refers to the law of action and the consequence of action which governs human consciousness. Karma states that good intent and good deeds contribute to good karma and a happier rebirth, while bad intent and bad deeds contribute to bad karma and a rebirth full of struggle. In classical Indian philosophy, karma drives the entire cycle of cause and effect, rebirth, and liberation (*moksha*). Concepts like saṃsāra (the cycle of rebirth) and mukti (freedom from the cycle) are closely tied to the doctrine of karma.

➡️ *We will explore each belief in greater detail shortly...*

1.4. The Historical Timeline

Main historical periods:

The history of Hinduism is often categorized into distinct periods of development. Although the early history of Hinduism is difficult to date with certainty, the following list presents a rough chronology.[4]

Before 2000 BCE
The Pre-Vedic Period

1500–500 BCE
The Vedic Period

500 BCE–500 CE
The Epic, Puranic and Classical Age

500 CE–1500 CE
Medieval Period

1500–1757 CE
Pre-Modern Period

1757–1947 CE
British Period

1947 CE–the present
Independent India

---

[4] Origins of Hinduism. https://www.edu.gov.mb.ca/

1.4.1. Pre-Vedic Period

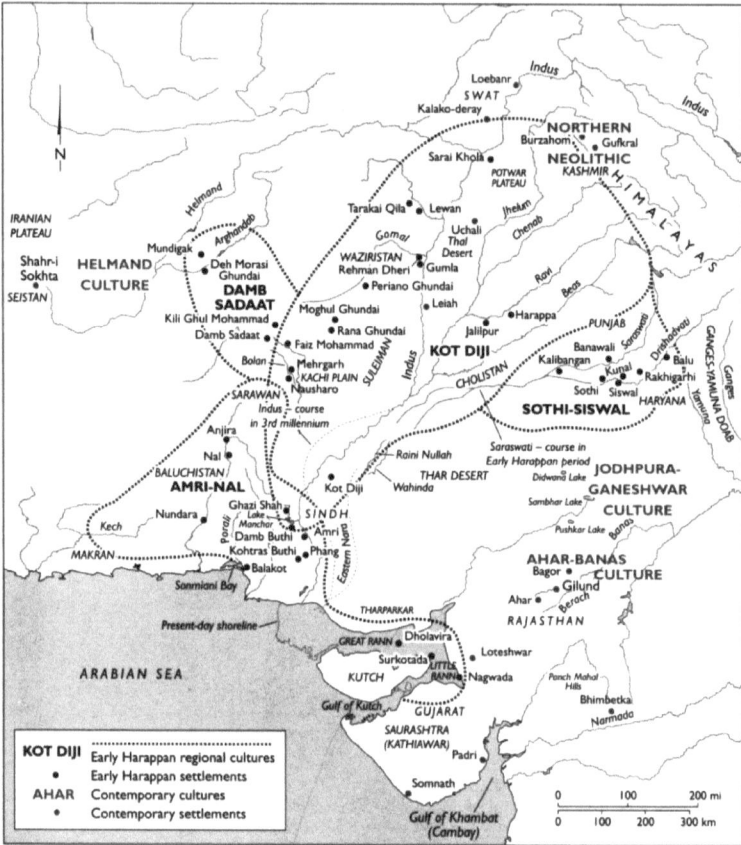

Figure 2 – The Greater Indus Valley 1900 BCE

Before 2000 BCE: The Pre-Vedic Period.

This period, which saw the development of urban planning, drainage systems, and impressive architectural structures, laid the groundwork for later cultural and religious advancements. The sophisticated city layout and standardized weights and measures indicate a high degree of social organization and governance.

As we delve into the pre-Vedic period, it's crucial to recognize the profound impact of these early practices on subsequent religious thought. Reverence for nature, fertility rituals, and burial customs reveal a society deeply connected to its environment and a belief system that viewed the divine within the natural world.

The earliest phase, known as the pre-Vedic period, includes the *Indus Valley Civilization (also called as Harappan Civilization)* and various local pre-historic religions. The Indus Valley Civilization, flourishing between 2600-1900 BCE in present-day Pakistan, was a highly developed culture that extended from the eastern Himalayas to Gujarat and near the Iranian border. The civilization, with major cities like Mohenjo-Daro and Harappa, developed independently without influence from other contemporary civilizations such as Sumer or Egypt. Evidence suggests that early Hindu practices may have originated in this culture, which faded by 1500 BCE. The Harappans seemed to believe that the divine was present within nature itself, rather than worshiping a creator God separate from the world. They focused on fertility, which they encouraged through rituals involving the worship of sexual symbols or organs. These practices are likely aimed at honouring a fertility deity or drawing on nature's powers to promote growth and creation. For them, the divine was closely connected to the natural world and expressed through its powerful forces, such as fertility and creativity. If they had a fertility deity, offerings or sacrifices may have been part of their rituals to seek favour.

The Harappan religion was figuratively represented. The existence of an elaborate polytheistic and naturalistic religious system suggests the presence of religious leaders, possibly rulers regarded as divine, priest-kings, or priests. Evidence from human skeletons suggests that the Harappans practiced burial rituals. Bodies were decorated with ornaments, possibly wrapped in cloth, and placed in wooden coffins with offerings in pots. Harappan religion was polytheistic, involved the worship of idols, and was closely connected to nature.

The Downfall

The Indus Valley Civilization came to an end around 2000-1900 BCE. Various factors have been suggested to explain the gradual decline and eventual collapse of urban life in the region, leading to the civilization's disappearance[5]. The Indus Valley Civilization remained hidden for nearly four thousand years until its ruins were uncovered by British and Indian archaeologists in the 1920s. Today, after nearly a century of excavation, it is considered the foundation of Indian civilization and possibly the origin of Hinduism.

1.4.2. Vedic Period

1500–500 BCE: The Vedic Period

Figure 3 - Vedic Period Teachings

The Vedic period began with the arrival of Indo-Aryan migrants around 1900 to 1400 BCE, introducing the Vedic religion, which forms the basis of Hinduism. There are differences of opinion regarding

---

[5] The roots of Hinduism by Asko Parpola. Oxford University Press.

whether the Aryans arrived, or whether they were the original inhabitants of the land.

The Vedic period is the earliest period of Indian history for which we have direct textual evidence, but even with this evidence, it is difficult to establish chronological periods or absolute dates within the period.

The transition from the pre-Vedic to the Vedic period is quite fascinating. The Harappan civilization, with its nature worship and fertility rituals, laid an important groundwork. When the Indo-Aryan migrants arrived, they brought with them new religious ideas that would form the foundation of Hinduism.

In the early Vedic period, people were mainly pastoral and had a great respect for natural forces like fire (Agni), the sun (Surya), and the sky (Indra). These elements were worshipped through rituals and sacrifices to maintain harmony and seek divine favour. The hymns of the Rig Veda from this time show a deep admiration for these natural elements and a quest to understand the world.

As time went on, the rituals became more complex, needing the expertise of the Brahmins, who eventually became the religious experts. This period also saw the creation of the Yajur Veda, Sama Veda, and Atharva Veda, which expanded the Vedic literature and offered detailed guides for various rituals.

The later Vedic period, also known as the "Brahmana" period, involved codifying these rituals in the Brahmanas. These texts not only explained the rituals but also introduced philosophical and theological discussions that set the stage for the Upanishads.

The Upanishads, written towards the end of the Vedic period, shifted the focus from rituals to deep philosophical questions about reality, the self (Atman), and the ultimate reality (Brahman). Concepts such as reincarnation, karma, and the pursuit of moksha (liberation) were explored, paving the way for the development of Hindu philosophy and spirituality.

There are two main theories regarding this period: the Aryan migration thesis, which suggests that these migrants became the dominant cultural force in the region, and the cultural transformation thesis offers that the Aryan culture developed from the existing Indus Valley culture.

During the Vedic period, the Brahmins were not yet recognized as a distinct community, and the caste system had not been established. The gods worshipped at that time were later replaced by deities with different names and forms[6].

By 1500–1200 BCE, the Rig Veda, one of Hinduism's most important texts, was written though some scholars suggest it could be even older, dating back to as early as 1900 BCE. Around 800 BCE, the Upanishads were composed, introducing key concepts such as reincarnation and karma. During this time, Buddhism and Jainism also emerged, diverging from mainstream Hinduism.

Vedic Scriptures:

The term "Veda" means "knowledge." The primary scriptures of the Vedic age were the four Vedas: Rig Veda, Yajur Veda, Sama Veda, and Atharva Veda. These texts were mainly collections of hymns sung or chanted during sacrificial rituals and were composed in Vedic Sanskrit. Later, additional texts such as the Brahmanas, Aranyakas, and Upanishads were added to each of these Vedas. In their original form, the four Vedas are known as the Samhitas (or Collections). It is believed that the Vedas were initially passed down orally and written down later. The original hymns were likely composed in Rhythmic structure [7].

The four primary divisions of the Vedas are as follows:

---

[6] James Talboys Wheeler, *The History of India from the Earliest Ages,*
Vol I: The Vedic Period and the Mahabharata (London: N. Trubner & Co,1867)
[7] The Rig Veda, http://www.utexas.edu/cola/centers/lrc/RV/ Accessed on April 24, 2015.

1. Samhitas: These are collections of metrical hymns, prayers, and songs typically sung or chanted during various rites and sacrifices.

2. Brahmanas: These are prose commentaries and theological discussions that explain the meanings of different texts, sacrifices, and ceremonies.

3. Aranyakas: Often referred to as the "forest texts," these works include both appended and independent commentaries and meditations by hermits (yogis) living in the forest, reflecting on the significance of the rituals and sacrifices outlined in the Vedic hymns.

4. Upanishads: Generally considered part of the Aranyakas or independent from them, the Upanishads explore mystical reflections on the nature of the world, soul, life, death, and reality, and the lack of a clear dividing line between them.

The four *Samhitas* are as follows:

1. Rig Veda
   Thus, the Rig Veda is referred to as the book of Praise-knowledge. It is structured into 10 books, called Mandalas, with each Mandala containing several hymns or Suktas.

2. Sama Veda
   The name Sama Veda comes from the word Saman, which means "melodies," making it the book of "knowledge of melodies." It is believed that the hymns in this text were primarily used during the Soma sacrifice ("act of willingly giving up something valued for the sake of a greater purpose or someone else's benefit"), with many hymns being repeated from the Rig Veda.

3. Yajur Veda
   The term *Yajus* means "sacrificial formula," so the Yajur Veda provides the "knowledge of sacrificial formulas." There are two main versions: the Shukla Yajur Veda (White Yajur Veda) and the

Krishna Yajur Veda (Black Yajur Veda). The White Yajur Veda emphasizes customary rituals and contains more explanatory material regarding the rituals[8].

4. Atharva Veda

The Atharva Veda is known as the book of the "knowledge of magic formulas" (*Atharvan*). It comprises a collection of spells, prayers, charms, and hymns, including "prayers to safeguard crops from lightning and drought, charms against venomous serpents, love spells, and healing spells." This text includes many verses, some taken from the Rig Veda.

Vedic Theology:

Throughout history, there have been numerous interpretations of Vedic theology. One of the most original perspectives was proposed by Scholar Max Muller (1823-1900), a prominent authority on the Sanskrit language and translator of several ancient texts. His expertise allowed him to compare religions both theologically and linguistically. In his work *Lectures on the Origin and Growth of Religion, as Illustrated by the Religions of India* (1878), Max Muller suggested that Vedic religion primarily centred around the worship of the Sky God or Heavenly Father.

Max Muller writes….

> Five thousand years ago, or, it may be earlier, the Aryans, speaking as yet neither Sanskrit, Greek, nor Latin, called him Dyu Patar, Heaven-father.
>
> Four thousand years ago, or, it may be earlier, the Aryans who had travelled southward to the rivers of Punjab, called him Dyaush-pita, Heaven-father.

---

[8] The Texts of the White Yajurveda, tr. by Ralph T.H. Griffith [1899]

> *Three thousand years ago, or, it may be earlier, the Aryans on the shores of the Hellespont, called him Ζευς πατηρ [Zeus pater], Heaven-father.*
>
> *Two thousand years ago, the Aryans of Italy looked up to that bright heaven above, hoc sublime candens, and called it Ju-pitar, Heaven-father.*
>
> *And a thousand years ago the same Heaven-father and All-father was invoked in the dark forests of Germany by our own peculiar ancestors, the Teutonic Aryans, and his old name of Tiu or Zio was then heard perhaps for the last time[9].*

Muller believed that the personification of natural elements eventually evolved into their deification (the act of making someone into God) as gods. For example, he noted that the name Dyaus (equivalent to Zeus or Jupiter, the light-giver, aptly associated with the sky) was later supplanted by various deities representing key activities of the sky, such as thunder, rain, storms, evening and morning, night, and day[10]. Consequently, a pantheon of deities gradually emerged in the Vedas.

James Wheeler[11] classified the more important Vedic deities as follows:

- Indra - God of the firmament (*rain*)
- Varuna - God of the waters
- Agni - God of fire. (*fire*)
- Surya - The sun.
- Soma, or Chandra - The Moon.
- Vayu - the god of wind. (*air*)
- Maruts - the breezes who attended upon Indra.
- Yama - The God or judge of death

---

[9] Max Muller, Lectures on the Origin and Growth of Religion as *Illustrated by the* Religions of India (London: Longmans, 1901), p.223.

[10] Ibid, p.218

[11] James Talboys Wheeler (1824–1897) was a British historian and civil servant renowned for his extensive works on Indian history, particularly focusing on the Vedic and post-Vedic periods of Hinduism

---

Vedic Worship:

There is no evidence of temples during the Vedic period, nor any record of idol worship in the Vedas. However, altars are mentioned. For Vedic priests, the altar was not just a simple structure instead it held cosmic significance—it represented the farthest edge of the earth, and the sacrifice performed on it was seen as the center of the world. Precise calculations were made to ensure its proper positioning, involving astronomical, geometrical, and mathematical principles. Some scholars have even suggested that intricate astronomical relations influenced the choice of the number of stones and pebbles placed around the altar.

This Upanishad is believed to have been written around the 7th century BC, offering insight into the philosophical mindset of the Vedic period. It strays from the karmic practices of Vedic religion and instead delves into mystical contemplations.

Quick Summary of the Vedic Period:

- Vedic religion appears to be polytheistic, with deities such as Indra, Mithra-Varuna, Surya, and Agni being prominent. However, there is evidence suggesting these deities were different names for the One God worshipped in the Vedas[12] .
- Vedic religion saw the gradual separation of Devas (gods) from the Asuras (anti-gods), who were later demonized.
- The caste system seems to have gradually developed during the Vedic period.
- Vedic sacrifices aimed to atone for sins, seek nature's blessings, ensure protection, and attain soul salvation.
- While the Brahmanas focus on karmic practices and provide detailed instructions for performing sacrifices through the Brahmins, the Upanishads view karmic religion as secondary and emphasize Self-realization as the path to true salvation.
- The quest in Vedic religion is for truth, light, and immortality.

---

[12] Rig Veda Verses 1.164.46

- There was a rise of the Brahmin class above the Kshatriyas, along with an intensification of sacrificial rituals and the Dakshina (offering) system.

1.4.3. Epic, Puranic, and Classical Age

Figure 4 - Hinduism Scriptures

500 BCE–500 CE: The Epic, Puranic and Classical Age.

Beginning around 500 BCE, this era witnessed the creation of key Hindu texts like the Epics and Puranas, which laid the groundwork for devotional Hinduism, centred around deities such as Shiva, Vishnu, and Devi. The rise of the Gupta Empire (320–500 CE) brought stability, enabling Hinduism to flourish and expand. Around 200 CE, Hindu laws were codified, leading to a revival of Hinduism as India's dominant religion, often called a "Hindu Renaissance."

From 500 BCE onward, the reverence of Indra, the primary deity of the Rig Veda, shifted to the worship of Vishnu, Shiva, and Devi. Vedic yajna (ritual sacrifice) was largely replaced by puja (devotional worship), while the speculative philosophies of Vedanta overshadowed the ritualistic Mimamsa school of thought. The focus shifted from the Vedas to the development of the Ramayana and the Mahabharata, two great epics written during this time. Although Vishnu had been a Vedic deity, his prominence increased, while God Shiva evolved from his earlier form as Rudra, and Devi emerged as a significant goddess, replacing earlier fertility goddesses.

During this period, the Mauryan Empire was established by Chandragupta Maurya and later expanded by Ashoka, who promoted Buddhism across much of India. Jainism also flourished. The second Gupta Empire (circa 319-490 CE) unified much of the Indian subcontinent, sparking a cultural renaissance in Hinduism and marking a golden age for traditional arts and sciences.

The Epics:

The "Epic Age" in India, spanning roughly from 1000 to 600 BCE, is named for the creation of significant epics such as the Ramayana, Mahabharata, and Upanishads. These works are not only religious and mythological texts but also vital components of India's historical roots. The Mahabharata, which includes the Bhagavad Gita, forms the ideological foundation of Hinduism, akin to the Bible in Christianity. These epics offer a vivid portrayal of ancient Indian society, which was largely rural, with rulers inheriting their positions and agriculture being the main economic activity. Arts, handicrafts, and pottery also thrived during this period.

The Ramayana, traditionally attributed to the sage Valmiki, and the Mahabharata, attributed to Vyasa, are monumental epics that capture the ethical, cultural, and spiritual essence of ancient India. These epics reflect the complexities of Dharma (righteous duty) and Artha (purpose), offering insights into the human condition and the divine interplay in mortal affairs.

The Ramayana narrates the life of Sri Ram Chandra, the prince of the Ayodhya Kingdom, who is exiled from his father's kingdom and embarks on an arduous journey with his wife Sita and brother Lakshmana. This journey culminates in the dramatic rescue of Sita from the demon king Ravana. The Mahabharata, on the other hand, encompasses a vast array of stories and characters, centralizing the Kurukshetra War and the philosophical discourse of the Bhagavad Gita. These texts serve not only as religious scriptures but also as extensive cultural repositories that have shaped Indian ethos and moral perspectives for centuries.

The Puranas, written in Sanskrit, further elaborated on the mythological narratives and rituals, encapsulating the ever-evolving dynamics of Hindu theology. These texts, along with the epics, played a significant role in the transition from Vedic ritualism to a more diverse and devotional form of Hinduism.

The epics detail the governance of society, with kings collecting taxes and holding supreme authority, while priests conducted rituals to deter malevolent forces. Over time, priests gained influence over kings due to their perceived connection with the gods. Warriors were trained to protect the kingdom, and while the caste system existed, it was not rigid—social mobility was possible, as warriors or outcastes could be adopted into the priestly class. The Dravidians (ethnic and linguistic group), who were deeply respected and feared, held a unique position in society. Recreational activities such as gambling, horse racing, and hunting were also popular during the Epic Age.

We will explore the caste system in greater detail throughout this book...

Great Epics of India:

The three great epics of India are the Srimad Bhagavat Gita, the Ramayana, and the Mahabharata. It is often said that understanding these epics is key to understanding India, as they have profoundly shaped the nation's culture. These epics have been a rich source of inspiration for poets and dramatists, offering legendary heroes and expressing timeless truths through their dramatic narratives.

The Srimad Bhagavatam tells the story of the divine child Gopala, who later becomes Krishna. It begins with the forces of evil, the asuras (demons), triumphing over the benevolent devas (deities) and taking control of the universe. Krishna, through a mix of peace and creative strategy, defeats the demons, restoring hope, justice, freedom, and goodness—a recurring theme in many Hindu legends.

The Ramayana, traditionally attributed to the sage Valmiki, recounts the life of Sri Ram Chandra, the prince of the Kosala Kingdom. The epic narrates his banishment by his father, King Dasharatha, his journeys through the forests of India with his wife Sita and brother Lakshmana, the abduction of Sita by Ravana, the demon king of Lanka, the subsequent war, and Rama's victorious return to Ayodhya to be crowned king.

The Mahabharata is a grand narrative centred on Krishna and the Kurukshetra War, detailing the destinies of the Kaurava and Pandavas princes. It also includes philosophical and devotional content, such as discussions on the four "goals of life." Notable sections of the Mahabharata include the Bhagavad Gita, the story of Damayanti, a condensed version of the Ramayana, and the tale of Rishyasringa, all of which are often considered significant works.

The Puranas:

The Puranas are religious texts written in Sanskrit and form an integral part of Hindu sacred literature, which also includes the Vedas, Brahmanas, Aranyakas, Upanishads, and the great epics. They serve as a foundational element of Indian culture, shaping the framework of Hinduism. The Puranas are a broad category of ancient Indian religious literature, encompassing myths and ritual traditions. They provide guidelines for ritual practices and contain numerous mythological stories involving various gods.

The Puranas revolve around five key themes:

1. The creation of the universe
2. The secondary creation following periodic destruction.
3. The gods and supernatural beings
4. The eras of humanity
5. The histories of the solar and lunar dynasties.

Difference between Vedas and Puranas:

- The Vedas are religious texts passed down orally, while the Puranas consist of stories and legends related to religion.

- Vedas are classified as Shruti scriptures, meaning they are based on what was "heard" through divine revelation. In contrast, the Puranas are Smriti, meaning they are based on what is "remembered."
- There are four Vedas in total—Rig Veda, Sama Veda, Yajur Veda, and Atharva Veda—whereas there are 18 major Puranas, 18 minor Puranas, and one Mahapurana.

1.4.4. Medieval Period

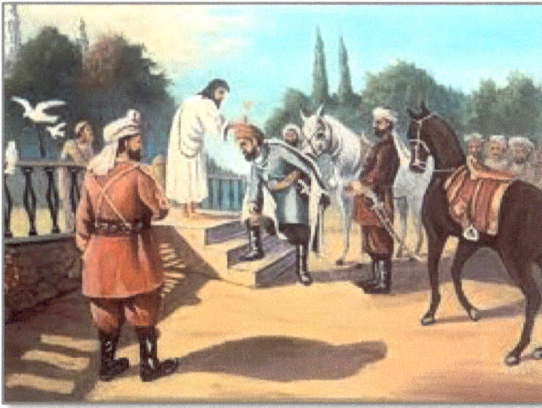

Figure 5 – Pictorial representation of the Medieval Period

500 CE–1500 CE: Medieval Period.

The medieval period in India extended from the fall of the Gupta Empire in the late 500s to the rise of the Mughal Empire in 1526. The Gupta Empire had dominated much of northern India, ushering in a golden age of culture and literature. Its collapse led to political fragmentation across the region. Throughout these thousand years, various dynasties competed to increase their influence over India. In the latter half of this millennium, Muslim forces from the West advanced into India, contributing to the decline of Buddhism and the rise of both Islam and Hinduism, which are now the largest religions on the Indian subcontinent. In the 1500s, the Mughal Empire emerged, conquering most of India before ultimately being overtaken by the British Empire.

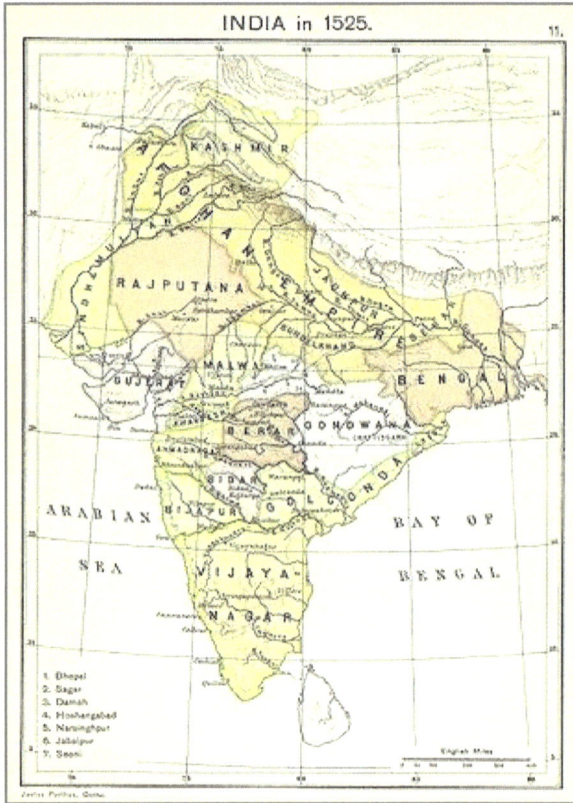

Figure 6 - Map of India in 1525

Numerous kingdoms and dynasties fought for power in medieval India. While some Buddhist kingdoms were present, most rulers adhered to Hinduism, which diminished Buddhism's influence. These kings not only supported art, architecture, and religion but also engaged in fierce warfare. For centuries, the Hindu kingdoms fought to gain control over the entire subcontinent but were largely unsuccessful. In the south, the Chola Dynasty expanded its reach beyond India by sea, conquering distant islands.

The power dynamics shifted with the arrival of Muslim invaders from the northwest, who moved swiftly across the subcontinent. The Delhi Sultanate emerged as the first significant Muslim polity in India and lasted for centuries. The Muslim presence in the north faced challenges from the Hindu kingdoms in the south, notably the Vijayanagara Dynasty, which would soon become the largest. In 1526, the Mughal Empire defeated the Delhi Sultanate, establishing control over all of India and marking the beginning of the modern era in Indian history.

The Bhakti Movement: A Religious Renaissance

After the decline of the Gupta Empire around 500 CE, Hinduism experienced notable changes. The Bhakti movement, which emerged between 800 and 1000 CE, focused on personal devotion to God and arose in response to Islamic influence and internal societal challenges. Adi Shankaracharya, born in 788 CE, introduced monotheistic elements to Hinduism. By the 7th century CE, Islam began to establish a presence in the Indian subcontinent.

Figure 7 - The Bhakti Movement in Hinduism

With the Gupta Empire's fall, regional kingdoms emerged, each supporting various religious traditions. For instance, the Cholas in the south endorsed Shaivism. This era saw the construction of grand regional temples, such as the Jagannatha temple in Puri (Orissa), and the Shiva temples in Chidambaram and Thanjavur (both in Tamil Nadu). These temples, dedicated to major deities, became centers of religious and political authority[13].

During this period, religious literature flourished not only in Sanskrit but also in spoken languages, especially Tamil. Poet-saints expressed their devotional feelings in these languages. Among the most renowned are the twelve Vaishnava Alvars (6th–9th centuries), which included a famous female poet-saint named Andal, and the sixty-three Shaiva Nayanars (8th–10th centuries). Later, prominent thinkers and teachers (acharyas or gurus) consolidated these teachings, developing new theological frameworks that were passed down through their spiritual lineages (sampradaya).

The Tantras also gained prominence, regarded as revelations that either complemented or surpassed the Vedas. While some tantric texts promoted practices considered ritually impure—such as offerings of alcohol, meat, and ritualized sexual acts to fierce deities—most of these texts focused on topics like daily and occasional rituals, temple construction, and cosmology.

---

[13] Professor Gavin Flood, BBC, August 24, 2009

Historical Overview:

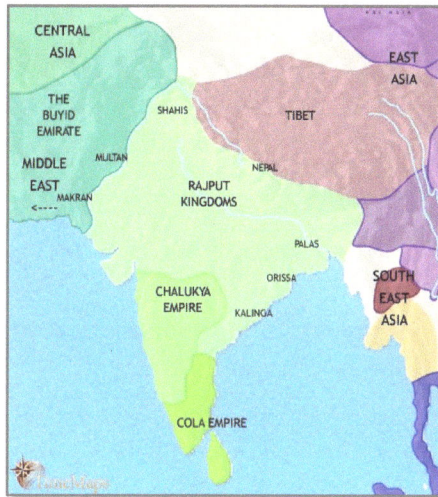

Figure 8 - Map of Medieval Period of India

Northern India

The Aftermath of the Gupta Empire

In the early 6th century, the once-mighty Gupta Empire began to crumble under the pressure of relentless raids by the Huns from Central Asia. By around 565 CE, the Gupta power had completely dissolved, leaving a fragmented landscape of numerous independent kingdoms vying for control in Northern India. This period of disunity and decentralization gave rise to regional dynasties, each striving to assert their dominance and preserve their cultural and political heritage.

These newly established kingdoms embarked on ambitious projects, constructing magnificent temples and fostering a renaissance in religious and cultural life. The decline of the centralized Gupta rule catalyzed the proliferation of localized power centers, each contributing to the rich tapestry of Indian history through their unique contributions to art, architecture, and governance.

Harsha Vardhana

In the first half of the 7th century, the political landscape of Northern India saw a brief period of unification under the dynamic leadership of Emperor Harsha Vardhana. Harsha, who ruled from 606 to 647, was a formidable warrior emperor and an astute statesman. From his capital in Kanauj, he launched ambitious military campaigns that brought vast territories under his control, effectively cementing his dominance over Northern India. However, despite his efforts to centralize power, the unity he fostered was short-lived. Following Harsha's death, his empire quickly disintegrated as regional vassal rulers seized the opportunity to reclaim their independence. Northern India once again fragmented into a mosaic of competing kingdoms, each striving to establish its authority and preserve its cultural heritage.

The Arab Invasion

In the early 8th century, Arab armies invaded the western regions of the Indian subcontinent. Motivated by the spread of Islam, the Arabs had already conquered vast territories including Iraq, Iran, Syria, Egypt, and North Africa, and they continued their expansion into Spain and India. The regions of Multan and Sindh became part of the Islamic Caliphate, leading to a lasting impact on the subcontinent. Over time, many in these areas converted to Islam, and Multan and Sindh would later become central to modern-day Pakistan.

The Struggle for Kanauj

The Gurjara-Pratihara kingdom emerged as a powerful force against further Arab advances into India. Their victories against the invaders elevated their status, and by the late 8th and early 9th centuries, they controlled Kanauj and dominated most of Northern India, except for the affluent Pala kingdom in the east. The city of Kanauj, once the capital of Harsha, symbolized imperial glory, and controlling it meant claiming supremacy over Northern India.

However, the Gurjara-Pratiharas faced challenges from the Pala dynasty of Bengal, which was notable for being the last major Buddhist dynasty in India and maintained ties with Buddhist states in

Southeast Asia. Under the Pala, the great university of Nalanda reached its peak.

Despite their prominence, the Pala also struggled to maintain lasting dominance. Over the next two centuries, three kingdoms—the Gurjara-Pratiharas in the northwest, the Pala in the northeast, and the Rashtrakutas in the Deccan—fought for control of Kanauj. The 9th and 10th centuries were marked by conflicts among these states, known as the "Tripartite Struggle," as all three held Kanauj at various times but never for long.

One result of this ongoing warfare was the rise of a warrior aristocracy known as the Rajput, who would establish several dynasties in subsequent periods. By the end of the 10th century, the political landscape was shifting; the Rashtrakuta dynasty fell in 973, and Gurjara power also began to decline. The Pala kingdom continued for another two hundred years but was unable to regain its earlier dominance.

Central India

The political landscape of Central India in the Deccan plateau saw significant shifts during the medieval period. Initially, the Chalukya dynasty ruled this region from the 6th century until the mid-8th century. Their reign was known for advancements in architecture, art, and culture.

However, their dominance ended when the Rashtrakutas rose to power, establishing a stronghold over the Deccan plateau. The Rashtrakutas were formidable rulers who made significant contributions to Indian art and literature, with their capital at Manyakheta becoming a notable center of culture and learning.

By the late 10th century, the Rashtrakuta dynasty declined, leading to the fragmentation of their empire into smaller states. These smaller states included the Western Chalukyas, Hoysalas, and Kakatiyas[14], each of whom played a crucial role in shaping the region's history. The

---

[14] Timemaps and The Hindus in Medieval India. Dr. Mahdi Husain. Agra.

Western Chalukyas revived the Chalukya legacy and ruled over parts of Karnataka and Maharashtra, while the Hoysalas were known for their exquisite temple architecture in Karnataka. The Kakatiyas, based in modern-day Telangana, were instrumental in the development of Telugu culture and literature.

This period of decentralization allowed for a rich interplay of culture, art, and regional politics, setting the stage for the later dynasties that would emerge in Southern India.

Southern India

By 500 CE, Southern India was dominated by three rival kingdoms: the Cheras, Pandyas, and Cholas. The Pallavas rose to power in the early 7th century and ruled until the late 9th century, after which the Pandyas briefly became the dominant force. The Cholas then gained control of Southern India from the early 10th century to the early 13th century.

The peoples of Southern India were active in maritime trade across the Indian Ocean, leading their rulers to seek overseas expansion, particularly in Sri Lanka. Although initial efforts were largely unsuccessful, the Cholas eventually established control over the northern part of the island in the 11th century and extended their influence as far as Southeast Asia[15].

Key Figures:

Key figures from the medieval period who continue to influence Hindu thought include:

1) Shankara (788–820), the founder of the prominent school of Advaita (nondual) Vedanta.
2) Ramanuja (1017–1137), the founder of Vishishtadvaita (qualified nondual) Vedanta.
3) Madhva, the founder of Dvaita (dual) Vedanta in the thirteenth century.

---

[15] The Hindus in Medieval India. Dr. Mahdi Husain. Agra.

4) Abhinav Gupta, recognized for his contributions to aesthetic theory.
5) Tulsidas (died in 1623), known for writing the Ram Charitramanas. Additionally, the
6) Nayanars (Tamil Shaiva poet-saints) and
7) Alvars (Vaishnava poet-saints) engaged popular audiences and ignited a religious revival from the fifth to the tenth centuries.

In the devotional tradition, figures such as:

8) Caitanya (1486–1533),
9) Basavanna (1105–1167),
10) Mira Bai (1516–1546),
11) Tukaram (died in 1649), and
12) Sant Gnaneshwar (thirteenth century) is also notable.

Shankara (780–820) travelled extensively, engaging and defeating scholars from unorthodox movements like Buddhism and Jainism, which had established significant centers of learning across India by the turn of the millennium. He reasserted the authority of the Vedic canon, promoted Advaita (monism), and laid the groundwork for the development of the Vedanta tradition.

Following Shankara, the Vaishnava philosophers Ramanuja (c. 1017–1137) and Madhva (thirteenth century) produced their scriptural commentaries, introduced new theological ideas, and established their lineages. Ramanuja built upon Shankara's ideas by qualifying his impersonal philosophy, while Madhva emphasized the existence of a personal God. During this same period, Shaivism also flourished, with important philosophers like Abhinav Gupta (c. 975–1025) writing commentaries on the Tantras, which were seen as an alternative revelation to the Veda, among other texts.

Hindus in the Medieval Period:

Hindus in medieval India freely practiced their religious rites, as seen in customs like Sati, sun-eclipse fairs, and bathing at ghats (steps leading to water). Temples and Dharamsalas (shelters for pilgrims) were built and maintained, with some still standing in places such as Vrindavan, Govardhan, Gaya, and Ranpur. In Vrindavan, four 16th-century temples remain. Govardhan, in Mathura district, houses the Hari Dev temple, built around 1500 A.D.

Moreover, historical records reveal that Emperor Ahmad Shah, who reigned from 1748 to 1754 A.D., issued documents confirming that some Muslim rulers provided grants for the maintenance and upkeep of Hindu temples. This gesture of patronage highlights a unique aspect of religious and cultural symbiosis during a period often marked by conflict and division. Such contributions played a crucial role in preserving the architectural and cultural heritage of Hinduism, ensuring that temples continued to serve as centers of worship and community life[16].

Society and Economy Developments:

During the medieval period, a new form of Hinduism evolved with new movements, sects, and philosophical schools that emphasized devotion (bhakti), mysticism, and philosophical reinterpretation.

The growing influence of Hinduism during the medieval period had a profound impact on Indian society. This new form of Hinduism, while distinct from the ancient Vedic religion, remained rooted in Vedic teachings and principles. The evolution of Hinduism saw the integration of various philosophical and theological ideas, which contributed to the richness of the religion's cultural and spiritual heritage.

This period also witnessed the establishment and flourishing of various religious institutions, temples, and places of worship, which became central to community life. The promotion of religious and philosophical discourse by figures such as Shankara, Ramanuja, and Madhva played a key role in shaping the intellectual landscape of the time. Their works not only reinforced Vedic authority but also

---

[16] The Hindus in Medieval India. Dr. Mahdi Husain. Agra.

introduced new dimensions to Hindu theology, which continued to influence the faith for centuries to come.

Simultaneously, Hindu practices and customs became more widespread and entrenched in daily life. The construction and maintenance of temples and Dharamsala provided spaces for communal worship and pilgrimage, contributing to the cohesive identity of Hindu communities across India.

Caste System

A key aspect of this rise was the enhanced status and authority of the Brahmin priestly caste, which came to be regarded as the foremost religious authority. Naturally, given their top position in the caste hierarchy, the Brahmins encouraged the division of castes. This trend was already evident during the Gupta Empire at the end of the ancient period, and throughout the medieval period, the caste system became increasingly pervasive and rigid as Hinduism spread.

Moreover, the system became more intricate, with hereditary occupational groups evolving into sub-castes, and inter-caste marriage increasingly frowned upon.

Status of Women

The status of women varied across time and regions in medieval India, but the general trend was a decline in their social and familial roles. Records indicate that some high-status women, particularly queens, were involved in governance and contributed to the arts, especially music and dance. Many temple dancers were well-educated and skilled in their crafts.

Conversely, both urban and rural women appeared to face greater restrictions in their daily lives. Widows have experienced a significant loss of status. Among high-caste women, the practice of sati— voluntary self-immolation on their husbands' funeral pyres—first recorded during the Gupta period, became widespread in these centuries.

> Sati (सती) was an ancient Hindu practice where a widow self-immolated on her husband's funeral pyre. It was considered an act of supreme devotion and purity, but over time, it became a forced or expected ritual in some communities, leading to social and ethical concerns. The practice is linked to the legend of Goddess Sati, who immolated herself in grief, though historical records show it was practiced among certain warriors and royal classes. It was seen as a mark of ultimate devotion and loyalty, but many Hindu scriptures do not mandate it.

Trade and Towns

International trade, particularly across the Indian Ocean and into Central Asia, brought many foreigners to medieval India, including Arabs, Persians, Chinese, and people from the Malay Peninsula. Persian Zoroastrians fleeing Muslim persecution in Iran settled in India, forming Parsee communities. Christian groups established themselves in the southwestern coastal ports, while Jewish communities had existed in various towns and cities since ancient times.

Large Muslim trading communities also emerged in Indian ports. During this period, Muslim merchants and sailors increasingly dominated the Indian Ocean trade. This shift was supported by changes within India itself; as Hinduism expanded and Brahmin teachings gained prominence, maritime trade became less acceptable for devout Hindus, who viewed it as polluting due to contact with foreigners, considered outcastes and ritually unclean.

Despite these changes, Indian Ocean trade grew during medieval times, which, in turn, stimulated internal trade. New trading towns emerged, such as *Shravanabelagola* in South India, which transformed from a religious settlement in the 7th century into a significant commercial center by the 12th century.

Other towns thrived as pilgrimage centers, which also fostered trade. Unlike ancient Hindu temples, which were typically small structures set in walled enclosures with open-air worship, medieval India saw the construction of massive temples that rivalled the wealthy

Buddhist monasteries (spiritual and religious institutions) of earlier eras.

These grand temples, supported by royal patronage, served multiple functions: religious, social, and judicial. Temple construction was both a commercial and religious endeavor, with merchants financing their construction to compete with royal temples. Additionally, shrines built by wealthy landlords in rural areas acted as centers of authority and trade, catering to the religious needs of agrarian communities. Large temples also employed hundreds of individuals across various guilds and professions.

Cultural Developments:

During medieval India, regional languages emerged as important mediums for literature. While Sanskrit had been the dominant language for the Brahmins in ancient India, dialects like Tamil and Kannada in South India became prominent for intellectual expression. The new Hindu cults' use of local languages for their sacred texts significantly contributed to their popularity, and even at royal courts, these regional languages began to replace Sanskrit[17].

However, Sanskrit still maintained its status as the main language of high culture. Like the Gupta period, works with intellectual aspirations or intended for widespread readership continued to be written in Sanskrit.

Literary productions during this time included poetry, grammar, dictionaries, manuals, rhetoric, commentaries on older texts, prose fiction, and drama. These works were typically written on palm leaves bound together like books.

Leading poets were influential figures in the courts of Indian rulers, and many noblemen, ministers, ascetics, and monks also contributed to the literary scene. Various poetic forms emerged, including *shatpadi* (six-line verses), *ragale* (lyrical compositions in blank verse), and *tripadi* (three-line verses). The traditional *champu*, which combined

---

[17] K. Majini Jes Bella, Vels University.

prose and verse, also continued to be popular, often performed with musical accompaniment.

Inscriptions on stone and copper plates were also prevalent, primarily in regional languages, though some were in Sanskrit or bilingual. Typically, the sections in bilingual inscriptions that described the king's title, genealogy, and origin myths were written in Sanskrit.

Local languages were commonly used in daily administration and commerce, including contracts and records of land ownership.

The End of the Medieval Period:

Medieval India is generally considered the period from the fall of the Gupta Empire to the rise of the Mughal Empire in the 16th century. This era witnessed significant changes in the subcontinent, including the evolution of modern Hinduism, the decline of Buddhism, and the rise of Islam as a dominant force. These religious shifts were accompanied by important developments in politics, social structures, the economy, art, architecture, and literature.

The Delhi Sultanate, which had briefly revived, came to an end when its last ruler was defeated at the Battle of Panipat in 1526 by Babur, who then founded the Mughal dynasty. This marked a new chapter in India's history, characterized not only by the emergence of a new imperial dynasty but also by external influences that began to reshape the region, including the introduction of firearms and the arrival of European traders along the Indian coasts. Over time, these traders would grow in influence and eventually gain control over the entire subcontinent[18].

---

[18] K. Majini Jes Bella, Vels University.

1.4.5. Pre-modern Period

Figure 9 - Pre-Modern Period. King Akhbar

1500–1757 CE: Pre-Modern Period.

The "pre-modern period" of Hinduism refers to the time before British colonialism, roughly from the 12th century to the early 19th century. This period saw important changes in religious practices, philosophical ideas, and cultural shifts in Hinduism.

Between 1400 and 1700, European colonization and the spread of Islam influenced Hinduism. The Hindu Renaissance began around 1600, with modern interpretations of sacred texts and social reforms. Mughal emperors like Akbar, known for promoting religious tolerance, attempted to unite Hindu and Muslim beliefs. Akbar supported Hindu scholars and artists, while his great-grandson *Aurangzeb*, who ruled from 1658 to 1705, restricted Hindu practices and destroyed temples. Under Mughal rule, Hindus were often excluded from public life, leading to a focus on personal spirituality and the rise of devotional (bhakti) movements, which emphasized love for God through song, poetry, and spiritual equality.

Islam's influence in South Asia began around the end of the first millennium when Arab traders arrived. Early interactions were mostly peaceful, but Muslim military campaigns also established Islamic rule in northern and central India. Islamic monotheism and rejection of idol worship sometimes caused religious conflicts, but there were also instances of cultural blending. Indian art from this period reflects a mix of South Asian and West Asian styles, creating a unique artistic tradition[19].

During the Mughal era, the devotional (bhakti) movements, particularly in Maharashtra and Punjab, flourished. Saints like Mirabai, Tukaram, and Surdas expressed their devotion through poetry, focusing on both a formless God (Nirguna) and a God with qualities (Saguna). This period also saw a mix of Hindu devotion, meditation, and Islamic mysticism[20].

Key developments during this time included:

The Mughal Empire (16th–18th century), where rulers like Akbar encouraged religious tolerance and dialogue between Hinduism and Islam. Akbar even founded a new religion, Din-i-Ilahi, which tried to combine elements of both.

The revival of Vedanta philosophy under spiritual leaders following *Adi Shankaracharya*, who helped maintain Hindu traditions.

In southern India, the Vijayanagara Empire (14th–17th century) promoted Hindu art, culture, and religion, while Rajasthan's Rajput kingdoms, built temples and supported Hindu scholars.

New religious sects emerged, such as *Gaudiya* Vaishnavism, led by *Chaitanya Mahaprabhu*, which focused on Krishna worship, and the Swaminarayan tradition.

Key Features:

- Regional Diversity: Different regions of India developed their unique expressions of Hinduism during this period, with distinct practices, deities, and rituals. The influence of regional

---

[19] The Hindus: An Alternative History" by Wendy Doniger
[20] India: A History" by John Keay

languages and cultures on Hinduism became more pronounced.

- Devotional and Personal Spirituality: The Bhakti movement brought an emphasis on personal devotion to God, shifting the focus away from Vedic rituals and Brahminical control over religious practices.
- Philosophical and Theological Debates: The period saw the crystallization of various Hindu philosophical schools, which engaged in deep debates over metaphysics, ethics, and theology.
- Impact of Political Power: Hinduism in this period was shaped by interactions with political power, whether under the Delhi Sultanate, Mughal rule or later the British. Religious practices adapted to these new realities, and in some cases, syncretic practices developed.

This pre-modern period of Hinduism was thus a rich and complex era, marked by significant religious, cultural, and social transformations.

1.4.6. British Period

Figure 10 - British Period

1757–1947 CE: British Period.

The British colonization of India, starting with the Battle of Plassey in 1757, brought about significant changes. Initially, the British allowed Hindus to freely practice their religion, but later missionary efforts led to religious conflicts. During this time, key Hindu leaders like *Ramakrishna Paramahansa* and *Swami Vivekananda* emerged, helping revive Hinduism and introducing it to the Western world.

Between 1757 and 1947, the British Empire gradually took shape in India, though this was not part of an early, deliberate plan. The British came to India as traders, not conquerors, but their involvement in Indian politics deepened as the Mughal Empire declined, leading to British dominance. By 1803, the British had taken control of Delhi, marking their firm hold over India. Although British rule brought education, technology, and democracy, it also imposed discrimination, racism, and cultural prejudice.

The British East India Company entered Indian politics due to the Mughal Empire's decline and regional instability. They capitalized on events like the Battle of Plassey in 1757 to expand their control. In response to the challenges faced by the Mughals, including the rise of regional powers like the Marathas and the Sikhs, British colonialism spread across the subcontinent.

Colonial rule reshaped Indian society, particularly through the introduction of individual property rights in the 1790s, which altered the class structure. The British also began codifying Indian religious practices, which led to the emergence of modern Hinduism. Reform movements, led by figures like *Rammohun Roy, Dayananda Saraswati*, and *Swami Vivekananda*, aimed to modernize Hinduism by emphasizing Vedic texts and aligning it more with Western notions of religion, such as monotheism and canonical scriptures. These reforms, influenced by Western ideas, played a key role in shaping Hinduism as it is perceived today and contributed to the rise of Indian nationalism.

When the British encountered the diverse religious practices in India, they tried to classify them within their understanding of religion, often misinterpreting them. Their critiques and the influence of

Western education led to various social reform movements. Reformers like *Rammohun Roy*, *Dayananda Saraswati,* and *Vivekananda* aimed to purify and modernize Hinduism by focusing on the Vedic texts and rejecting practices like image worship. Although these reformers were Indian, their ideas were shaped by Western thought, influencing how Hinduism is viewed today, particularly in terms of its emphasis on texts and structured religious practices.

The caste system in India, which traces its origins back to the Vedas, has been a deeply rooted and longstanding social structure. Although it has faced opposition throughout history, it consistently served the interests of those in power, which helped maintain it with little change over the centuries. However, the arrival of the British brought Western education and new employment opportunities, particularly for the emerging middle class. This shift allowed more lower-caste individuals, including Dalits, to access education. A pivotal figure in the fight for Dalit rights was *B.R. Ambedkar,* whose efforts played a key role in challenging caste discrimination.

? *Does this help clarify the impact of British rule on the caste system and Ambedkar's role in advocating for Dalit rights? Let me know if you'd like to explore any part of this further!*

The final area of interest in how the West influenced the shaping of Hinduism is the rise of the Hindu nationalist movement, known as Hindutva. Before colonial rule, there was no unified concept of India as a single nation; people identified themselves by their region or religion, such as being Bengali, Tamil, Saiva, Jain, or Muslim. It was British rule that fostered a shared identity among the indigenous population, where the term "Indian" came to refer to the native inhabitants. A key figure in this movement was *Vinayak Damodar (Vir) Savarkar*, who in 1923 published a book on Hindutva ("Hinduness"), in which he defined what it means to be a true "Hindu." His work focused not on religion but on promoting a particular form of nationalism.

Since India's population had never seen itself as a unified whole, and under colonial rule, *Vir Savarkar* believed the country had been "invaded" and needed to be reclaimed. His concept of Hindutva went beyond religion, encompassing cultural, racial, and geographical elements. He broadly defined a Hindu as someone who considered India their sacred land, a definition that excluded Muslims and Christians but included almost everyone else, even the Indian diaspora. In 1925, influenced by *Savarkar's* ideas, *Kesham Baliram Hedgewar* founded the nationalist organization Rastriya Swayamsevak Sangh (RSS), later led by Madhav Sadashiv Golwalkar. The RSS drew from various ideologies, notably from Hitler and the Nazi Party, which it admired as a cultural project and used to promote racial, cultural, and religious paranoia (mental state). Over time, the RSS came to embody a radical form of right-wing Hindu nationalism[21].

In all these aspects, we can see how the influence of the West—whether through critiques of Indian traditions, Western education, or the clash between Western and Indian ideas—sparked various social reforms in India. These reforms were largely reactions to Western influence. Looking back at the changes that took place during British colonial rule, Hinduism, as we understand it today, is quite different from its earlier form. The British presence led to a restructuring of Hinduism, shaped primarily by Western ideas, and even resulted in the creation of the term "Hinduism." This term unified the diverse populations of India, at least theoretically, under a single religious and cultural identity, despite having little grounding in historical reality. The version of "Hinduism" studied today is largely a product of British colonial rule. However, this influence wasn't one-sided—Indian culture, particularly in regions with Indian diasporas, has also shaped Western culture. The widespread popularity of yoga and the incorporation of Indian religious imagery into Western popular culture are prime examples of this cross-cultural exchange[22],[23].

---

[21] Majumdar, R.C. ed. 1965. 'History and Culture of the Indian people', vol.10 pt. II. Bombay: Bharatiya Vidya Bhavan.

[22] Beltz, Johannes. 2008. 'Ambedkar, Bhimrao Ram (1891-1956).' In Encyclopedia of Hinduism, eds. Denise Cash, Catherine Robinson, and Michael York. New York: Routledge.

[23] Ram-Prasad, C. 2003. 'Contemporary Political Hinduism.' In The Blackwell Companion to Hinduism, ed. Gavin D. Flood. Oxford: Blackwell Publishing.

1.4.7. Modern Period

Figure 11 - Post Indian Independence Period

The–the present: Independent India. The modern Period is also called as Post-Indian Independence period.

After India gained independence in 1947, Hinduism continued to evolve. The partition of India led to widespread violence and lasting impacts on the religion. In the following decades, Hindu beliefs were codified into Indian law, and the Hindu diaspora established vibrant communities around the world. The modern period has seen increased recognition of LGBT rights and the role of women in Indian society, with Hinduism continuing to adapt to contemporary challenges while maintaining its ancient traditions.

The Hindu concept of dharma played a significant role in influencing the Indian independence movement by providing a moral and ethical framework for the leaders and participants. Dharma, as a concept deeply rooted in Indian philosophy and religion, emphasized principles of duty, righteousness, and social order, which guided the actions of individuals during the movement. Leaders like *Mahatma Gandhi* drew upon the idea of dharma to justify nonviolent resistance and civil disobedience as morally superior methods of protest. Additionally, the inclusive understanding of kinship ties and social order within the concept of dharma, as exemplified by figures like *Vidur* in the Mahabharata, provided a basis for unity and solidarity among diverse groups striving for independence. Overall, the Hindu concept of dharma infused the Indian independence movement with a sense of moral purpose and collective responsibility, shaping its strategies and outcomes.

Ending the Colonial Era

On August 15, 1947, India's first Prime Minister, *Jawaharlal Nehru*, declared, "At the stroke of midnight, while the world sleeps, India will wake to life and freedom." This marked the end of two centuries of British colonial rule, freeing 370 million people. However, independence came with the tragedy of Partition, as Pakistan was created as a separate Muslim-majority nation with 70 million people. Pakistan had two parts: West Pakistan, near Afghanistan, and East Pakistan (now Bangladesh) by the Ganges Delta. Around 15 million people moved between India and Pakistan, leading to violent clashes that killed over a million. India's independence also inspired the global anti-colonial movement, freeing many countries in Asia and Africa in the years that followed.

Hindu nationalism emerged in the 19th century during India's fight for independence from British rule. After India gained independence in 1947, it became less prominent but reemerged in the 1980s. Since 2014, it has grown significantly and become a mainstream ideology in India. While Hindu nationalism has many layers, its focus is shaping India based on Hindu values and traditions

Hinduism Today

Hindu nationalists continue to take the ideas of figures like *Savarkar* and *Golwalkar* seriously. They argue that Hinduism is too diverse, and complex compared to monotheistic religions like Christianity and

Islam. Unlike those religions, Hinduism lacks a single, universally accepted religious text or a strict code of conduct and has many deities instead of one God worshipped by all Hindus. This diversity, they believe, historically weakened Hindu unity, making it difficult to effectively resist invasions by Muslims and British colonialists. To address this, Hindu nationalists have worked to promote "Hindutva" through cultural reconstruction, aiming to create a stronger, unified Hindu identity by organizing the religion around shared beliefs.

In recent years, Hindu nationalism has risen significantly in India. After independence in 1947, Prime Minister Jawaharlal Nehru and his Indian National Congress (INC) government promoted secularism, pushing Hindu nationalism into the background for a time[24].

1.5. Hinduism, Buddhism & Jainism

Figure 12 - Symbol of Religions

Hinduism, unlike Buddhism, did not originate from the teachings of a single founder. It encompasses a wide array of traditions, reflecting its evolution over more than 5,000 years. Many practices within Hinduism share roots with the ancient traditions of Buddhism, which originated in India in the 5th century BCE. The caste system in Hindu Dharma likely contributed to the rise of Buddhism, which emerged in response to the dominant religious practices of Brahminism. Buddhism, founded by *Siddhartha Gautama* (the Buddha) in the 6th or 5th century BCE, contrasts with Hinduism in having a single founder and texts centred on the Buddha's teachings[25].

Although Buddhism shares certain terminology with Hinduism, such as the concept of "Dharma," their interpretations differ. In Hinduism, Dharma refers to the cosmic order and the reasons for existence, while

---

[24] Allahabad: The Name Change that killed My City's soul. BBC.
[25] The Center for Public Art History, Dr. Melody Rod-ari.

in Buddhism, it signifies the teachings of the Buddha. In Hinduism, salvation is achieved by realizing the unity of the individual soul with Brahman, whereas Buddhism denies the self and teaches that enlightenment and nirvana, or the cessation of suffering, are attained through understanding the true nature of reality and escaping the cycle of rebirth known as samsara[26].

For around 2,500 years, Hinduism and Jainism have coexisted in South Asia, sharing a long history of interaction and mutual influence, particularly in philosophy and mythology. However, as a minority group (currently making up only 0.5 percent of India's population), Jains have historically paid more attention to Hindus than vice versa. Up until the 12th or 13th centuries CE, Hindus generally regarded Buddhists as their main religious rivals. This perspective is evident in both primary and secondary sources, with much of the material on Hindu-Jain intersections coming from Jain texts or scholars of Jainism[27].

The traditions of Jainism were primarily upheld by a lineage of 24 tirthankaras, or spiritual teachers, with *Vardhamana Mahavira* being the most prominent and the last in this succession. *Mahavira* was likely a contemporary of *Gautama Buddha*, and both emphasized self-discipline, meditation, and asceticism as the path to salvation. Their teachings often contrasted with those of the Vedic priests, who focused on ritual practices and their role as mediators between humanity and the divine[28].

The three religions have emerged from the same source, which is called the Aryan Truths. So, all three believe in the karma theory, the cycle of birth & rebirth and a destination of infinite peace and happiness which is the goal of every individual (known variably as Moksh, Nirvana, Kaivalya). Thus, the fundamentals of the three religions are the same.

---

[26] Asia Society, https://asiasociety.org/

[27] Hinduism and Jainism, Jonathan Green. DOI: 10.1093/obo/9780195399318-0048

[28] Pew Research Center, Kelsey Jo Starr.

1.6. Hinduism Denominations

Hinduism encompasses many sects, with four often recognized as the major denominations; Shaivism, Vaishnavism, Shaktism & Smartism.

For over 200 years, Western scholars have grappled with understanding Hinduism, a faith that, to outsiders, appears to allow followers to arbitrarily choose among a dozen gods as the Supreme Being. This religion is marked by its immense diversity in beliefs, practices, and forms of worship. Some Indologists have categorized the Hinduism they encountered as polytheistic, while others have introduced terms like henotheism to explain its perplexing array of spiritual traditions. However, few have recognized—let alone articulated—that India's Sanatan Dharma, or "eternal faith," known today as Hinduism and encompassing nearly 1.2 billion adherents, is a family of religions with four main denominations: Saivism, Shaktism, Vaishnavism, and Smartism.

Understanding these distinctions is crucial for accurately comprehending and conveying the essence of Hinduism. Contrary to common misconceptions, all Hindus worship one Supreme Being, albeit by different names. For Vaishnavites, Lord Vishnu is the ultimate God; for Saivites, it is Siva; for Shaktas, Goddess Shakti holds that position; and for Smartas, who are more liberal, the choice of deity rests with the individual devotee.

Each denomination boasts its diverse lineages of gurus, religious leaders, priesthoods, sacred texts, monastic communities, pilgrimage sites, and tens of thousands of temples. These denominations include a broad spectrum of worship practices, rituals, and theological interpretations, each contributing to the multifaceted tapestry of Hinduism. Vaishnavism, for example, places a strong emphasis on devotion (bhakti) to Lord Vishnu and his avatars, such as Krishna and Rama. This tradition is marked by vibrant temple worship, singing of hymns, and elaborate festivals.

Shaivism, on the other hand, centers around the worship of Lord Shiva, known as "The Destroyer." Followers engage in deep meditation, yoga, and temple rituals to achieve spiritual oneness with Shiva. This sect's rich philosophical texts and ancient traditions underscore the pursuit of moksha (liberation) through self-discipline and ascetic practices.

Shaktism uniquely venerates the Divine Feminine in the form of Goddess Shakti, representing both nurturing and fierce aspects. Shaktas engage in diverse rituals, from chanting and holy diagrams (yantras) to awakening the kundalini energy within. This tradition often complements Shaivism, emphasizing the dynamic interplay between the male and female divine principles.

Smartism, the most liberal of the major denominations, advocates a more eclectic approach, allowing worshippers to choose their preferred deity among the five major ones: Ganesha, Shiva, Shakti, Vishnu, and Surya. This sect promotes the philosophy of oneness and the unity of all paths leading to the same ultimate truth.

Despite their divergent beliefs, each sect functions as a complete and independent religion. Nonetheless, they share a profound cultural and spiritual heritage that includes concepts such as karma, dharma, reincarnation, the all-pervasive Divine, temple worship, rituals, numerous deities, the guru-disciple tradition, and the Vedas as their authoritative scriptures. This shared heritage binds the various strands of Hinduism into a cohesive spiritual tradition, rich in diversity yet unified in its core principles.

Understanding these nuances allows for a deeper appreciation of Hinduism's complexity and its enduring relevance in the lives of millions of adherents around the world.

Shaivism is one of the largest branches of Hinduism, with followers who worship Lord Shiva, often referred to as "The Destroyer," as their supreme deity. Originating in southern India, Shaivism has spread to Southeast Asia, including Vietnam, Cambodia, and Indonesia. Like other major Hindu sects, Shaivism reveres the Vedas and Upanishads as sacred texts. Devotees worship in temples and practice yoga, striving to achieve oneness with Shiva.

Figure 13 - Lord Shiva in Meditation

Saivism is ancient and truly timeless, with no definitive beginning. It serves as the foundation of the multifaceted religion we now know as Hinduism. Scholars trace the origins of Siva worship back over 8,000 years to the advanced Indus Valley civilization, yet sacred texts indicate that Saivism has always existed. Modern history identifies six primary schools of thought within Saivism: Saiva Siddhanta, Pashupatism, Kashmir Saivism, Vira Saivism, Siddha Siddhanta, and Siva Advaita. The richness and beauty of Saivism are evident in its practical culture, enlightened understanding of humanity's role in the cosmos, and profound system of temple mysticism and Siddha yoga. It offers insights into the soul's journey from God and back to God, emphasizing the unfolding and awakening of the soul under the guidance of enlightened sages. Like other sects, it consists mainly of devoted families led by hundreds of orders of swamis and sadhus, who pursue the passionate, world-renouncing path to moksha.

The Vedas state, "By knowing Siva, the Auspicious One hidden in all things, as subtle as the film that rises from clarified butter, the One who encompasses the universe—through the realization of God, one is freed from all bondage." - Aum Namah Sivaya[29].

Shakti is God Siva's inseparable power and manifest will, energy or mind. Lord Siva is pure love and compassion, immanent and transcendent, pleased by our purity and sadhana. There are no divine earthly incarnations of the Supreme Being. God Siva is one with the soul. The soul must realize this advaitic (monistic) Truth by God Siva's grace.

Vaishnavism is the largest Hindu sect, with an estimated 640 million followers globally. This denomination includes well-known sub-sects such as Ramanism and Krishnaism. Vaishnavism recognizes several deities, including Lord Vishnu, Lakshmi, Krishna, and Rama, with religious practices varying across regions in the Indian subcontinent. Vaishnavites are primarily dualistic and deeply devotional, with a rich tradition of saints, temples, and scriptures.

Figure 14 - Lord Vishnu in Celestial Splendor

Worship of Lord Vishnu, meaning "pervader," dates to Vedic times. The Pancharatra and Bhagavata sects gained popularity before 300 BCE. The 5 Vaishnava schools we recognize today were established

---

[29] Satguru Sivaya Subramuniyaswami's Dancing with Siva.

during the Middle Ages by Ramanuja, Madhva, Nimbarka, Vallabha, and Chaitanya. Vaishnavism emphasizes prapatti, or single-pointed surrender to Lord Vishnu and his many incarnations, known as avatars. Key devotional practices include japa, ecstatic chanting, and dancing, collectively known as kirtana. Temple worship and festivals are celebrated with great elaboration. Philosophically, Vaishnavism spans from Madhva's pure dualism to Ramanuja's qualified nondualism, and Vallabha's nearly monistic perspective. In this tradition, God and the soul remain eternally distinct, with the soul's ultimate destiny, through divine grace, being to worship and enjoy God forever. Although generally nonascetic and advocating bhakti as the highest path, Vaishnavism is supported by a vibrant monastic community. Its central scriptures include the Vedas, Vaishnava Agamas, Itihasam, and Puranas. The Bhagavad Gita states, "To those who meditate on Me and worship with an undivided heart, I grant the attainment of what they do not have and preserve what they already possess.[30]" - Aum Namo Narayanaya.

There are parallels wherein the divine consorts are conceived as the inseparable powers of Lord Vishnu and His incarnations: e.g., Krishna's Radharani and Rama's Sita. Lord Vishnu is loving and beautiful, the object of man's devotion, pleased by our service and surrender. Lord Vishnu has ten or more incarnations. God and soul are eternally distinct. Through Lord Vishnu's grace, the soul's destiny is to worship and enjoy God.

Shaktism is unique among the major Hindu traditions in its worship of a female deity, the goddess Shakti (also known as Devi). Shakti embodies both gentle and fierce aspects. Shaktas use chants, rituals, holy diagrams, yoga, and even real magic to invoke cosmic forces and awaken the kundalini energy within. While some Shaktas practice monotheism by worshiping Shakti alone, others venerate multiple goddesses. This female-centred tradition is sometimes seen as complementary to Shaivism, which emphasizes a male supreme deity.

---

[30] Bhagavat-Gita

Figure 15 - Shaktism Goddess

While the worship of the Divine Mother predates recorded history, Shakta Hinduism emerged as an organized sect in India around the fifth century. Today, it manifests in four distinct forms: devotional, folk-shamanic, yogic, and universalist, each invoking the fierce power of Kali or Durga, or the gentle grace of Parvati or Ambika. Devotional Shaktas perform puja rites, particularly using the Shri Chakra yantra, to cultivate a close relationship with the Goddess. Shamanic Shaktism incorporates magic, trance mediumship, firewalking, and animal sacrifice for purposes such as healing, fertility, prophecy, and empowerment. Shakta yogis aim to awaken the dormant Goddess Kundalini and unite her with Siva in the Sahasrara chakra. Shakta universalists embrace a reformed Vedantic tradition, as exemplified by *Sri Ramakrishna*. "Left-hand" tantric practices go beyond conventional ethical boundaries. Shaktism is predominantly advaitic, emphasizing the soul's ultimate destiny as complete oneness with the Unmanifest, Siva. The central scriptures include the Vedas, Shakta Agamas, and Puranas. The Devi Gita proclaims, "We bow down to the universal soul of all. Above, below, and in all four directions, Mother of the universe, we bow.
- "Aum Chandikayai Namah".

Shakti is an active, immanent being, separate from a quiescent and remote Lord Siva. The Goddess Shakti is both compassionate and terrifying, pleasing and wrathful, assuaged by sacrifice and submission. The Divine Mother is incarnate in this world. The Divine Mother, Shakti, is a mediatrix, bestowing advaitic moksha on those who worship Her.

Smartism is a more orthodox and selective tradition within Hinduism, primarily followed by members of the Brahmin upper caste. Smartas worship five deities: Vishnu, Shiva, Devi, Ganesh, and Surya. The *Sringeri* temple is the central place of worship for this denomination. Smartism follows a philosophical and meditative path, focusing on the understanding of man's oneness with God.

Figure 16 - Lord Ganesha

Figure 17 - Lord Surya

Figure 18 - Sringeri Temple, Sringeri, Karnataka. India.

Smarta refers to a follower of classical smriti, particularly the Dharma Shastras, Puranas, and Itihasam. Smartas venerate the Vedas and respect the Agamas. Today, this tradition is closely associated with the teachings of *Adi Shankara*, the monk-philosopher known as Shanmata Sthapanacharya, or "founder of the six-sect system." He worked throughout India to unify the diverse Hindu faiths of his time under the Advaita Vedanta philosophy. To promote a cohesive approach to worship, he popularized the ancient Smarta Five-Deity altar, which includes Ganapati, Surya, Vishnu, Siva, and Shakti, adding Kumara as well. Devotees can select their "preferred Deity," or Ishta Devata, with each God representing a reflection of the singular Saguna Brahman. Shankara organized hundreds of monasteries into a ten-order, dashanami system, which now features five main pontifical centers. He authored extensive commentaries on the Upanishads, Brahma Sutras, and Bhagavad Gita. Shankara stated, "It is the one Reality that appears to our ignorance as a manifold universe of names, forms, and changes. Like gold from which many ornaments are crafted, it remains unchanged in essence. Such is Brahman, and That art Thou." Aum Namah Sivaya.

Shakti is a divine form of Ishvara. It is God's manifesting power. Ishvara appears as a human-like Deity according to devotees' loving worship, which is sometimes considered a rudimentary, self-purifying practice. All Deities may assume earthly incarnations. Ishvara and man are Absolute Brahman. Within Maya, the soul and Ishvara appear as two. Jnana (wisdom) dispels the illusion.

Paths of Attainment:

Saivism: In Saivism, the path consists of four progressive stages: charya (moral living), kriya (temple worship and devotion), yoga (internalized worship and meditation), and jnana (wisdom). The soul evolves through karma and reincarnation, moving from instinctual living to virtuous practices, ultimately reaching union with God Siva through the grace of a Satguru. Saivism values both devotional practices (bhakti) and meditative practices (yoga).

Shaktism: Shaktism shares similarities with Saivism but emphasizes God's Power more than God's Being. It incorporates the use of mantras and yantras, and it embraces dualities like male-female and pleasure-pain. Some sects follow "left-hand" tantric practices, using worldly experiences to transcend them, while the "right-hand" path is more traditional and conservative.

Vaishnavism: Vaishnavites view religion primarily as bhakti sadhanas, or devotional practices, believing they can connect with and receive grace from the Gods through the darshan (sight) of their icons. The paths of karma yoga and jnana yoga lead to bhakti yoga. Key practices include chanting the holy names of Vishnu's incarnations, especially Rama and Krishna. Liberation from samsara (the cycle of reincarnation) is achieved through complete surrender (prapatti) to Vishnu, Krishna, or his beloved consort Radharani.

Smartism: Smartas, the most eclectic Hindus, believe moksha (liberation) is attained through jnana yoga, which focuses on intellectual study and meditation without kundalini practices. The stages of jnana yoga include scriptural study (Shravana), reflection (manana), and meditation (dhyana). With guidance from a realized guru, the initiate meditates on their identity as Brahman (Absolute Reality) to overcome the illusion of Maya. Additionally, Smartas can pursue bhakti yoga, karma yoga, and raja yoga as paths to cultivate devotion, gain good karma, and purify the mind, which can also lead to enlightenment.

※

As we've seen, Hinduism encompasses four major sects or denominations: Saivism, Shaktism, Vaishnavism, and Smartism. While there are some differences among them, they share many similarities. All four traditions believe in karma and reincarnation, as well as a Supreme Being who exists in both form and formlessness, creating, sustaining, and destroying the universe in endless cycles. They all emphasize the importance of temple worship, recognize the three worlds of existence, and acknowledge the many gods and devas that inhabit them.

They agree that there is no inherent evil in the cosmos, which is created from and permeated by God. Each sect believes in Maya (though their interpretations vary) and sees the liberation of the soul from rebirth, known as moksha, as the ultimate goal of life. They also uphold dharma and ahimsa (non-injury) and believe in the necessity of a Satguru to guide the soul toward Self-Realization.

Devotees mark their foreheads with the sacred Tilaka, though each sect has its distinct symbol. Additionally, they typically prefer cremation after death, believing that the soul will take on a new body in the next life. While Hinduism has a wide range of sacred texts, all sects regard the Vedas and Agamas as the highest authorities, even though their Agamas may differ slightly. Here's a brief comparison of these four denominations.

Comparison:

Major Scriptures:
- Saivism: Vedas, Saiva Agamas and Saiva Puranas.
- Shaktism: Vedas, Shakta Agamas (Tantras) and Puranas.
- Vaishnavism: Vedas, Vaishnava Agamas, Puranas and the Itihasam (Ramayana and Mahabharata, especially the Bhagavad Gita).
- Smartism: Vedas, Agamas and classical smriti—Puranas, Itihasam, especially the Bhagavad Gita, etc.

Regions of Influence:
- Saivism: Strongest in South and North India, Nepal and Sri Lanka. Shaktism: Most prominent in Northeast India, especially Bengal and Assam.
- Vaishnavism: Strong throughout India, North and South.
- Smartism: Most prominent in North and South India.

Spiritual Practice:
- Saivism: With bhakti as a base, emphasis is placed on tapas (austerity) and yoga. Ascetic.
- Shaktism: Emphasis is on bhakti and tantra, sometimes occult, practices. Ascetic-occult.
- Vaishnavism: Emphasis is on supreme bhakti or surrender, called prapatti. Generally devotional and nonascetic.
- Smartism: Preparatory sadhanas are bhakti, karma, raja yoga. The highest path is through knowledge, leading to jnana.

1.7. Hinduism Caste System

The origins and evolution of India's caste system are complex. In early Indian society, especially during the Vedic period, people could choose jobs based on their skills and interests, guided by karma rather than heredity. Over time, however, the system became rigid, with the Brahmins emphasizing birth as the main factor for caste identity. This shift led to professions being passed down from father to son, making caste mobility nearly impossible. The Brahmins, at the top of the hierarchy, used various methods to reinforce caste divisions, impacting everything from daily life to burial practices. This transformation from a karma-based to a birth-based system has had deep social, economic, and cultural effects, leading to social fragmentation, mistrust, and conflicts that persist today[31].

---

[31] Prabin Kumar Yadav, B.A.LL. B Scholar Purbanchal University.

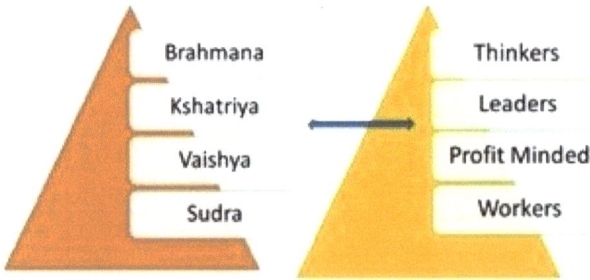

Figure 19 - Caste System in Hinduism

The caste (varna) system is a social hierarchy in India that categorizes Hindus based on their karma (actions) and dharma (duties). While the term "caste" is of Portuguese origin, it is commonly used to describe the Hindu concepts of *varna* (colour or social class) and *Jati* (birth group). Many scholars believe this system has existed for over 3,000 years.

The four primary castes, ranked by prominence, are:

1. Brahmins: Intellectual and spiritual leaders
2. Kshatriyas: Protectors and public servants of society
3. Vaishyas: Skilled producers
4. Shudras: Unskilled laborers

Caste System in Ancient India

Around 1500 BC, nomadic warriors known as Aryans began settling in northern India. Their horseback riding skills allowed them to conquer local populations and expand southward into the subcontinent. The Aryans brought their beliefs, customs, and writing system, Sanskrit, with them. They created songs and stories about their gods called the Vedas. For hundreds of years, these stories were passed down orally until the Aryans developed their writing system around 500 BC. This period, from about 1500 BC to 322 BC, is known as the Vedic Age. During this time, the Aryans established a strict social hierarchy known as the caste system.

At the top were the Brahmins, the priests who held significant power. They alone could study and teach the Vedas and perform religious sacrifices. Because of their authority, people from other castes often gave them generous gifts, believing this would lead to rewards in their next lives. Next were the Kshatriyas, the warriors and rulers who made daily decisions for the civilization, although their authority could be challenged by Brahmins. They could learn the Vedas but could not teach them. Kshatriyas were trained in military skills like archery and combat. The Vaishyas were skilled farmers, craftsmen, and merchants responsible for agriculture and trade. They could learn the Vedas but were not allowed to teach them. The Shudras included unskilled workers who had little education.

The existence of caste divisions in ancient Aryan society has been debated. The Indian Aryas believed that in the Satya Yuga, a time of purity, there was no caste, discrimination, or inequality. However, in the later Treta Yuga, as regional communities began practicing penance like the Brahmins, texts like Valmiki's Ramayana suggest that sages, including Manu, saw no distinction between Brahmins and these communities. This led to the formation of the four-caste system. This indicates that the Varnashram system did not originate in the Satya Yuga (a time of equality) but in the Treta Yuga (an agricultural feudal period).

The *Lingapurana* scripture states that the Varnashram system did not exist at first and was introduced in South India during the Treta Yuga. This suggests that the Chaturvarna system came later, with early Indian Aryan society initially having only two varnas. This supports the idea that early humans were part of the same race. As society's needs evolved, classification expanded from two to three, and eventually to four varnas. Historical evidence shows this gradual increase in varnas.

From a cultural perspective, the Aryans, who migrated into the Indus Valley and India, were distinct from the creators of the *Mohenjo-daro* civilization. The Aryans were less advanced and mainly nomadic pastoralists. Over time, they spread across India, following their cattle herds, and shifted from a nomadic lifestyle to agriculture, forming settled communities. Their lineage mixed with the indigenous people of the region (Anarya).

Around 1000 B.C., the use of iron in India marked a key development. Iron axes and spades allowed the clearing of forests and the digging of canals, making the Ganges Plain arable. This marked the beginning of India's agricultural era, which brought significant changes to labour and social structures[32].

Cultural Shift

As productivity increased, wealth grew, and more productive activities took place, slavery began to emerge. This shift marked the start of society's division into two main groups: masters (those who owned slaves) and slaves (those who were exploited).

This trend of dividing labour and society was seen across agricultural civilizations, including places like Yunnan, Mesopotamia, India, and China. For example, in ancient China, society was divided into four main classes: Atharva (priests), Rathestha (warriors), Bastrophsuchanta (farmers, traders, herders), and Huiti (slaves). Similarly, ancient Europe had four classes: aristocrats, clergy, free farmers (peasants), and slaves.

In India, as the division of labour grew, class divisions started to form, gradually replacing the caste system as the state emerged. Around 1000 BC, India saw the rise of a slave state, with kings, armies, officials, and kingdoms ruled by lords who often oppressed slaves.

---

[32] Valmiki Ramayana Uttarkanda: (74/11-15), Varnashram System Ch Treta Prabhuti Suvrata: Bharate Dakshine Annual System Netreshyath. Lingapurana, Purvadha (89/95), Brahmadaranyaka Upanishad: 334.11-13, Sec. Tokareb, History of Religions, (Moscow Progress Publications, 1989), p. 212, Thapar, Prev., p. 38, Fyodor Korodikan, Introduction to Ancient World History (Moscow: Pragati Publications, 1982). B.C. 13, Dr. D. Premapati (Indian Scholar), Antavantana, Parity, (Year 4, Extract 4, 2054), p. 6

Indian society was divided into two main classes: the Arya (ruling class) and the Dasa (enslaved indigenous people). The Rigveda describes these two classes in detail. The Aryas was further split into three groups: priests, rulers, and merchants/farmers. The Dasa class consisted of people conquered by the Aryas.

As a result, the state established a four-class system, which became the foundation of society. These four classes called 'Varnas' in the Rigveda, represented the key parts of the state and were symbolized as different parts of a cosmic being, or "virat purusha."

Bases of Caste Division

The main foundations of caste division in Indian society are as follows[33]:

1. Based on Purushasukta
2. Based on Skin Color
3. Based on Profession
4. Based on Quality (Guna)
5. Based on Birth or Descent

Demolishing a Myth in Hinduism Caste System

Evidence from ancient scriptures suggests that Hinduism—both its Vedic and classical forms—did not support the caste system and actively opposed it both in principle and practice. Even after the caste system emerged, Hindu society experienced significant occupational and social mobility. Furthermore, Hinduism created legends to highlight the caste system's invalidity, a notion that was bolstered by

---

[33] Friedrich Engels, The Family, Private Property and the Origins of the State (Moscow: Pragati Publications, 1986 | Kela and Thakur, vol., p. 65, Rahul Sankrityayan, Philosophy-Direction. | Shastri, Prev., p. 245, Baral, Prev., p. 176 133. Agenda, p. 176, Lokana tu vivarddyartham mukhabahuspadabradatah brahmin regional vaishya shudra cha niravatam yat | Mahabharata Shantiparva, verses 1-2, Janaklal Sharma, Our Society A Study, Prasad, East, BC. 34 142. Rigveda | Manusmriti: 10|80, Manusmriti: 1|9|1, Rigveda: 9|11|2|3

numerous reform movements throughout history. Despite this opposition, the caste system persisted due to various socio-economic and ecological factors that helped maintain balance among communities in a pre-modern world[34].

Vedic and classical Hinduism not only does not endorse the caste system but has also made significant efforts to oppose it in both principle and practice, clearly indicating that the caste system is not an inherent aspect of Hindu texts, philosophy, or practices. It will demonstrate that the caste system emerged and persisted due to entirely different factors unrelated to Hinduism. In Hinduism, the classification of human beings was purely done to diversify their work and responsibilities, and it was never intended to divide people based on their caste.

Caste System During British Colonization

The caste system during British Colonization was to divide people based on their religion and this system has nothing to do with the Philosophy of Vedic Hinduism. The caste system in India became a prominent issue during British rule. Before the British Raj, caste existed as a social tool but did not dominate Indian life. This study explores how the British altered the caste system, making it a central aspect of Indian society. It explains how the caste system gained significant importance and became deeply embedded in every social sphere. British manipulation of the caste system transformed Indian society in ways that cannot be undone.

Before British rule, the caste system was not as dominant, though it was used in various ways for administration and social control. Historians argue that the British exploited the caste system to its fullest extent. For example, people from lower castes were often seen as so impure that physical contact with them was considered

---

[34] Radhakrishnan, S (1994; first publication 1953): The Principal Upanishads, Harper Collins, New Delhi. Dumont, Louis (1999, first published 1970): Homo Hierarchicus: The Caste System and Its Implications, Oxford India Paperback, New Delhi.

humiliating for higher-caste individuals. The British, once settled, invested resources in formally categorizing castes into a ranked system to strengthen their imperial control. While the caste system may have had roots in earlier Brahmanical thought, the British did not improve it; instead, they deepened its rigidness, expanding its influence across Indian society.

The British made caste more rigid and immobile, formalizing its role in society and politics, which led to endless conflicts. The British highlighted caste distinctions, making caste appear as the only path to power and influence in Indian society. Scholars like *Bayly* (2000) and *Guha* (2003) argue that British rule shaped the modern political and social understanding of caste. Before British colonization, the caste system was more flexible, but the British made it more entrenched and divided, impacting people's behaviour across all areas of life—religion, economy, and society.

The caste system cannot be fully explained just by purity and impurity, as *Louis Dumont*[35] (1980) suggested that British rule redefined it. *Rao* (1989) pointed out that Brahmins' cooperation with the British helped them gain influential positions and trust. This led to the dominance of Brahmanical thinking in British India. *Waligora* (2004) agrees, noting that Brahmins gained significant power, influencing British perceptions of caste and its importance[36].

Recent Developments

In recent decades, conflicts related to the caste system in India have significantly increased. These disputes mainly occur in three areas: between higher Hindu castes and scheduled castes, between Hindus and Muslims, and between Hindus and Sikhs. All of these are part of

---

[35] Louis Dumont (1911–1998) was a French sociologist and anthropologist who made significant contributions to the study of the Hindu caste system through his book "Homo Hierarchicus" (1966).
[36] International Journal of Development Research, Vol. 11, Issue, 12, pp. 52678-52683. Rimsha Javed. University of the Punjab Lahore, Pakistan.

broader ethnic conflicts. The concept of ethnicity, introduced by *Max Weber* in 1958, helps explain these tensions. Ethnicity is a label used to categorize different groups within the caste system, regardless of their race, customs, or beliefs. The key point here is how ethnicity affects social dynamics.

Weber believed the caste system reflected different closed groups, and the main issue was the interaction between these groups, particularly regarding their struggle for status and power. As *Jackson* (1982) interpreted Weber's theory, "Ethnically isolated groups live in mutual repulsion and disdain. First, social discrimination and dishonour occur between independent groups. This leads to the development of a sense of inferiority, making political and economic exploitation possible."

Subordination causes political and economic exploitation and oppression. These two factors feed into each other, causing harm to large groups of people. The conflict between higher castes and scheduled castes is marked by violence and the fight for power and control in society. In recent years, changes in India's social structure have led to social movements and shifts in group rankings, which have further strained relations between ethnic divisions.

Conclusion

Before the British invasion, the caste system in India was not rigidly defined by fixed social or economic statuses. However, the British attempted to reshape Indian society based on the class system they had in their own country. To make things more manageable, British officials formalized the caste system and integrated it into the rules of governance, making it more rigid and unchanging. While the caste system is often seen negatively, some scholars acknowledge that it also has positive aspects. For example, it helped bring order to society, promoting mutual agreements and reducing rivalry among people[37].

---

[37] Aryal, A. 2021. Socio-political Dynamics of the Hindu Caste System. Bandyopadhyay, S. 1990. Caste, Politics, and the Raj, 29-30. Bayly, S. 2000. French anthropology and the Durkheimian in colonial Indochina. Modern Asian Studies,

1.8. Hinduism Beliefs

Earlier in the chapter on the History of Hinduism, we touched on the 7 Core Beliefs of Hinduism. Let's now explore these in greater detail.

7 Core Beliefs of Hinduism

- Belief 1. One Universal Soul
- Belief 2. Atman
- Belief 3. Samsara
- Belief 4. Scriptures (e.g. Vedas)
- Belief 5. Cyclical Time
- Belief 6. Dharma
- Belief 7. Karma

1.8.1. Concept of Universal Soul (परमात्मा)

Brahman (परमात्मा) Is the Universal Soul

Hindus believe in a universal soul or God called Brahman, which is the ultimate reality and divine essence that exists everywhere. Brahman can take on many forms, and some Hindus worship these forms as gods or goddesses. There is also a part of Brahman within each person, known as the Atman. Hindus believe in reincarnation, meaning that the soul (Atman) is eternal and lives many lifetimes, moving from one body to another.

To understand Brahman, think of it like the ocean. Just as the ocean is vast and contains everything within it, Brahman is the underlying essence of everything in the universe. The soul, or Atman, is like a drop of water from that ocean—separate in appearance, but ultimately part of the same whole. When a person achieves Moksha (spiritual

---

34(3), 581-622. | Bearce, G. D. 1961. British attitudes towards India, 1784-1858 (p. 51). London: Oxford University Press.

liberation), their soul returns to Brahman, just as a drop of water returns to the ocean.

The Upanishads explain that Brahman is beyond description—eternal, all-knowing, and the source of everything. It is the invisible force that creates, sustains, and connects all life. Though we may feel separate from Brahman due to our individual experiences, this separation is an illusion. Once we realize this, we can be freed from ego, reincarnation, and suffering.

In simple terms, Moksha means reuniting the soul (Atman) with Brahman, the universal soul, much like a drop of water merging back into the vast ocean.

Figure 20 - Representation of Moksha

1.8.2. Concept of Atman (आत्मा)

Atman (Soul) - The True Self

The term "Atman" comes from the Sanskrit word meaning "inner self" or "internal." Atman refers to the eternal and immortal soul, a core belief found in ancient texts like the Upanishads, the Bhagavad Gita, Jainism, and Ayurveda. Think of Atman as the essence of who you truly are, beyond the mind and body, much like the sun that remains constant even when hidden by clouds.

Figure 21 - Atman - The Soul

The Bhagavad Gita provides a lot of insight into the nature of the soul (Atman) and its liberation from the mortal world. The soul is neither born, nor does it ever die; nor having once existed, does it ever cease to be. The soul is without birth, eternal, immortal, and ageless. It is not destroyed when the body is destroyed[38].

In the Upanishads, Atman is seen as the central truth, representing pure consciousness and the eternal, unchanging part of us. It is often equated with Divinity itself. For example, the *Brihadaranyak* Upanishad says, "The supreme Divinity is the ultimate goal of the soul," and the *Aitreya* Upanishad mentions that God existed before the universe was created.

Atman is distinct from the body and mind, much like the root of a tree that remains stable while the branches (our body and mind) grow and change. It is the non-material self that never alters, unaffected by external attributes like race, gender, or nationality.

In Hinduism, Atman is closely connected to Brahman, the universal spirit or ultimate reality. The Upanishads teach that Atman (the soul) and Brahman (the universal spirit) are the same, like a drop of water that is part of the vast ocean. While individual souls are countless, they

---

[38] The Bhagavad-Gita. Chapter 2.

all share an eternal relationship with the Divine, even though they may be clouded by Maya or worldly illusions.

Some philosophies in Hinduism, like certain forms of yoga, suggest that by spiritual practices, one can realize their Atman, or true self, much like rediscovering a hidden treasure. Other views hold that the Atman within each person reflects Brahman, the universal spirit. When Atman and Brahman unite, spiritual liberation (moksha) is achieved, like how a river merges with the ocean.

Atman and Brahman are like two sides of the same coin, foundational to Indian philosophy. Atman is the individual soul, and Brahman is the cosmic soul—both essential to understanding the deeper principles of life. The Upanishads describe this relationship as the core of existence: Atman as the inner reality of individuals, and Brahman as the universal truth that connects everything[39] [40] [41] [42].

The following passage explains in metaphorical terms the idea that Atman and Brahman are the same:

> "As the same fire assumes different shapes When it consumes objects differing in shape, so does oneself take the shape of every creature in whom he is present." (Katha Upanishad II.2.9)

1.8.3. Concept of Samsara

Before understanding Samsara, it's important to grasp three key concepts: Dharma, Karma, and Moksha.

---

[39] Saraswati, Swami Prakashanand. (2001). The True History and Religion of India. Delhi: Motilal Banarsidas.

[40] Hiriyanna, M. (1995). The Essentials of Indian Philosophy. Delhi: Motilal Banarsidas.

[41] Saraswati, Swami Prakashanand. (2001). The True History and Religion of India.

[42] Radhakrishnan, S. and Charles A. Moore. (1997). A Source Book in Indian Philosophy. Princeton University Press.

Dharma refers to one's duty or path in life. Every living being has specific responsibilities and obligations, and following this righteous path is called fulfilling your Dharma. Karma is the idea of cause and effect, meaning that every action has consequences, whether good or bad. Moksha is the ultimate liberation—escaping the cycle of reincarnation and uniting with Brahman, akin to reaching spiritual freedom or "Heaven."

Figure 22 - Samsara Illustrated

Now, Samsara is the cycle of reincarnation, where after death, the soul is reborn into a new body, continuing in a cycle of life, death, and rebirth. The goal in Hinduism is to break free from this cycle by achieving Moksha, which happens when the soul is reunited with Brahman. To reach Moksha, one must follow Dharma and accumulate good Karma.

In simpler terms, Dharma is about fulfilling your role in life, and by doing so, you gather good Karma. If you live according to your Dharma, you'll build up good Karma, which will lead to a better situation in your next life. For example, if you're born as a beggar, Hinduism teaches that you should accept your role (Dharma) and live a virtuous life to build up good Karma. As a result, in your next life, you may be born into a better position.

Figure 23 - Picture Illustrating Good Karma

There are enormous ways to accumulate good karma in Hinduism, showcasing positive actions like helping others, speaking the truth, practicing non-violence, selfless service, meditation, and respecting nature.

To summarize, following your Dharma leads to good Karma, which helps you climb the spiritual ladder towards Moksha. Over time, Hindus have developed various practices to follow Dharma, build Karma, and deepen spirituality. These practices are known as Yoga. While the most familiar form, Hatha Yoga, focuses on the unity of mind and body, there are many different forms of yoga, each aimed at spiritual growth—whether through knowledge, devotion, or other means. All forms share the common goal of enhancing spiritual awareness.

☑ In the upcoming chapters, we will dive deeper into the concepts of Dharma and Karma.

The Upanishads offer many paths to attain Moksha. Let's explore each one.

Paths to achieve Moksha:

1. The path of knowledge: Jnana-Yoga
   Spiritual knowledge -leading to the knowledge of the
   relationship between the soul (atman) and God (Brahman)

2. The path of meditation: Dhyana-yoga
   The idea is to concentrate so you can reach the real self
   within you and become one with Brahman

3. The Path of Devotion: Bhakti-yoga
   Choosing a particular god or goddess and worshipping them
   throughout your life in actions, words and deeds.

4. The path of good work: Karma-yoga
   This involves doing all your duties correctly throughout your
   life.

1.8.4. The Scriptures (धर्मग्रंथ)

Figure 24 – Rishi holding Hinduism Scripture

Hinduism encompasses a vast array of ancient religious texts and oral traditions that convey timeless truths, many of which are believed by Hindus to have been divinely revealed or realized by enlightened sages. Key texts, including the Vedas, Upanishads, Agamas, and Puranas, along with epics like the Bhagavad Gita and Ramayana, lawbooks, and various philosophical works, have been transmitted through both oral and written traditions over generations. These ancient texts are called Scriptures of Hinduism.

⟹ *In the upcoming book, we will dive deeper into each Scripture.*

1.8.5. Concept of Cyclical Time (चक्रीय समय)

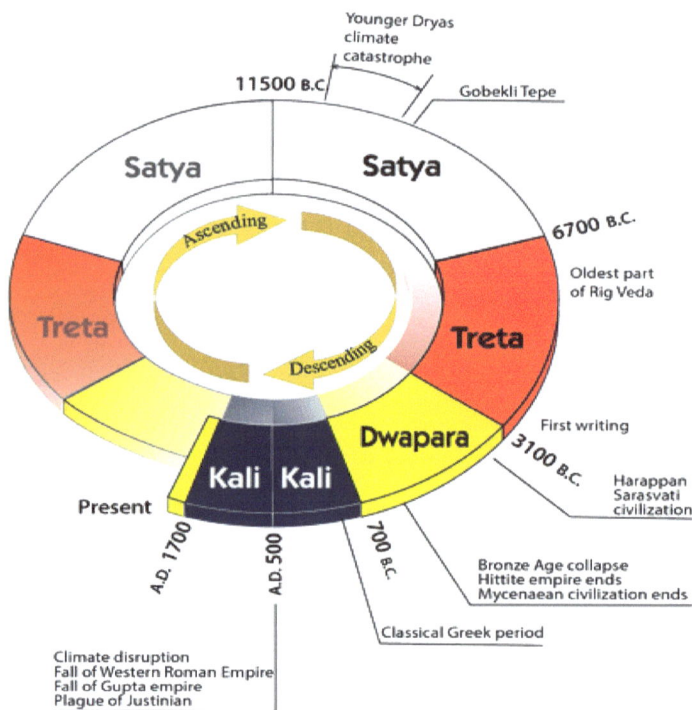

Figure 25 - Cyclical Time Illustrated

The Hindu concept of time is cyclical, not linear, and is best represented by the doctrine of the four ages or Yugas. Time is divided into four great epochs, each representing different qualities and stages of existence. These ages repeat in a continuous cycle of creation, decline, and rebirth, much like the changing seasons.

According to Hindu tradition, the universe passes through these four Yugas over millions of years. A complete Yuga cycle, known as a Kalpa, spans approximately 4.32 million human years. These Yugas are:

Satya Yuga (Krita Yuga) – Lasting 1,728,000 years, this is the age of truth and purity. It's said that righteousness (Dharma) was at its peak, and human beings lived in harmony with nature and the divine.

Treta Yuga – Spanning 1,296,000 years, this is when truth began to decline. Righteousness diminished by one-fourth, and people started experiencing a gradual loss of virtue.

Dvapara Yuga – Lasting 864,000 years, in this age, half of the truth was lost. The world became more materialistic, and conflict started to rise.

Kali Yuga – The current age, which began in 3102 B.C., will last 432,000 years. It is characterized by widespread dishonesty, strife, and a further decline in morality, with only one-fourth of righteousness remaining.

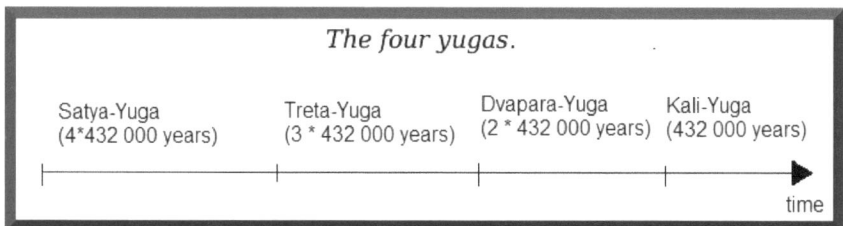

The four yugas.

Satya-Yuga (4*432 000 years)	Treta-Yuga (3 * 432 000 years)	Dvapara-Yuga (2 * 432 000 years)	Kali-Yuga (432 000 years)

time →

An easy way to visualize this is to think of the Yugas as the four seasons. Satya Yuga is like spring, full of growth and balance, while Kali Yuga is like winter, where darkness, conflict, and decay dominate. However, just as winter is followed by spring, the Yuga cycle continues, meaning that after Kali Yuga, the universe will be renewed and begin again with Satya Yuga.

In this cycle, each Yuga reflects a gradual decline in spiritual purity. For example, in Satya Yuga, truth and righteousness were absolute. By the time we reach Kali Yuga, evil and dishonesty are more prevalent. This cyclical view of time contrasts with the Western idea of linear progression, where time moves forward with a clear beginning and end.

To better understand these Yugas, imagine a lamp burning brightly (Satya Yuga) but gradually dimming until only a flicker of light remains (Kali Yuga). Eventually, the cycle renews, and the light shines brightly again[43].

In the following sections, we will explore each Yuga in greater detail.

1) Satya-Yuga

Figure 26 - Satya-Yug Period

---

[43] Dr. Vineet Aggarwal, Mumbai. India.

Satya Yuga, often called the "Golden Age," is a time when humanity is guided by the most benevolent gods, and everyone exhibits the purest and most ideal behaviour. In this era, intrinsic goodness reigns, making it the most balanced and ideal period in human history.

It is the first and most important of the four Yugas, characterized by wisdom, knowledge, and spiritual practices like meditation and penance. People in Satya Yuga were free from evil, deceit, and selfish desires. There were no divisions of class, caste, or creed, and everyone was treated equally. Hatred, conflict, and worldly desires were absent, leading to a life without sorrow, disease, or decay.

Humans in this era had remarkable strength, and longevity, and were deeply connected to meditation. According to Vedic texts, people lived up to 100,000 years. There was no cultural disparity, and everyone lived in harmony with nature, enjoying worldly comforts without conflict or competition. As time passed, however, people began to drift away from spirituality and sought more material comforts, leading to the rise of competition. This shift marked the transition to Dvapara Yuga, where the class-based society of varnashrama emerged.

2) Treta-Yuga

In Treta Yuga, the Silver Age, human beings engage in nonviolent religious sacrifice as a means of propitiating the gods and ultimately pleasing the Supreme Person, Vishnu. According to Hindu philosophy, the *Yugas* denote four distinct ages of mankind. The *Treta Yuga* is the Sanskrit name given to the second of the four Yugas. Translated, the term means "three collections." The Treta Yuga lasted for 1,296,000 years and saw important events such as the appearance of agriculture and mining. Three avatars of Lord Vishnu were said to appear during this Yuga: Vamana, Parashurama and Rama as the fifth, sixth and seventh incarnations, respectively.

Figure 27 - Treta Yug Period

During this era, the power of mankind was diminished as people became less spiritual and more focused on material possessions. Wars broke out frequently and climate changes became commonplace, giving rise to deserts and oceans.

Despite these seemingly negative effects, the Treta Yuga also brought knowledge of universal magnetism. This knowledge allowed humans to understand the forces of nature and the true nature of the universe.

In Treta yuga, human beings were extremely dutiful, moral, and compassionate toward their fellow living beings. They lived life spans up to 10,000 years. Although there was some division in society, it was nevertheless a time of overarching peace and prosperity.

Bhagavad Gita: Chapter 3, Verse 10.

सहयज्ञाः प्रजाः सृष्ट्वा पुरोवाच प्रजापतिः |

अनेन प्रसविष्यध्वमेष वोऽस्त्विष्टकामधुक् || 10 ||

saha-yajñāḥ prajāḥ sṛṣṭvā purovācha prajāpatiḥ
anena prasaviṣhyadhvam eṣha vo 'stviṣhṭa-kāma-dhuk

Sri Krishna Explains:

> In the beginning of creation, Brahma created humankind
> along with duties, and said, "Prosper in the performance of
> these *yajñas* (sacrifices), for they shall bestow upon you all
> you wish to achieve."

3) Dvapara-Yuga

Figure 28 - Dvapara Yuga Period

Before Dvapara Yuga began, at the end of Treta Yuga, people
started to stray from dharma, or the righteous way of life.
Individuals across all levels of society from Brahmanas to Sudras
exploited their positions for personal gain, often at the expense of
others. As conflicts arose, kings fought for power, wealth, and
influence. Unable to perform collective sacrifices, people turned to
worshiping Vishnu in his deity form. Many temples were built for
the worship of Vishnu and other demigods like Indra, Agni, and
Shiva.

During Dvapara Yuga, or the Bronze Age, selfishness and irreligion began to overshadow humanity's inherent godly nature. Trust in leaders and fellow citizens declined, but many righteous kings still upheld justice and virtue. People lived up to 1,000 years during this period.

The Dvapara-Yug talks about the life and times of Lord Krishna, the ninth avatar of Lord Vishnu[44]. This Yug ended when Lord Krishna completed his mission and returned to his original abode at Vaikuntha. By the end of Dvapara Yuga, Mother Earth became burdened by corrupt leaders who had abandoned spirituality for selfishness and violence. She took the form of a cow and sought help from Brahma, the universal creator. Brahma then appealed to Vishnu, who revealed that Krishna would descend to Earth to defeat the evil kings and restore virtue. This was when Krishna appeared and delivered the Bhagavad Gita to Arjuna.

4) Kali-Yuga

Shortly after Sri Krishna departed to His realm in the spiritual sky, Kali Yuga emerged with full force, disrupting the social order. Instead of guiding and protecting the people, religious and political leaders abandoned virtue and became the primary wrongdoers in society.

During Kali Yuga, or the Iron Age, spirituality and morality have faded significantly. Deception and hypocrisy masquerading as religion have become commonplace. This age is the opposite of Satya Yuga, with the world nearly devoid of peace. All living beings face material struggles just to survive, burdened by fear.

In Kali Yuga, people typically live up to only 100 years.

---

[44] Bhagavat-Gita

Figure 29 - Kali Yug Period: Yug of Destruction

The Bhagavata Purana describes human beings of Kali Yuga as follows:

> *"In this iron Age of Kali men almost always have but short lives. They are quarrelsome, lazy, misguided, unlucky and, above all, always disturbed." (Srimad Bhagavatam, 1.1.10)*

We are currently said to be living in Kali Yuga, a time marked by impurities and vices. The number of people with noble virtues is steadily declining. This age is characterized by floods, famine, war, crime, deceit, and duplicity. However, scriptures suggest that it is during this time of great turmoil that true liberation can be achieved.

Kali Yuga consists of two phases: In the first phase, humans, having forgotten the knowledge of their higher selves, were aware of the "breath body" separate from the physical self. Now, in the second phase, even this understanding has faded, leaving us focused solely on the gross physical body. This shift explains why people are now more concerned with their physical existence than any other aspect of life.

Our fixation on our physical bodies and lower selves, coupled with our pursuit of materialism, has led to Kali Yuga being called the Age of Darkness—an era where we have lost connection with our inner selves and are engulfed in profound ignorance[45].

It is widely believed in Hinduism that at the end of Kali Yuga, the last avatar of Lord Vishnu, known as Kalki, will appear to restore Dharma in the world. Kalki will represent the peak of human evolution, after which Pralaya, or destruction, will occur. Humanity will face extinction, leading to a reset of the Yuga cycle, and Satya Yuga will begin anew.

Teachings from the Scriptures:

Both great epics—the Ramayana and the Mahabharata—address the Kali Yuga. In the Tulasi Ramayana, the sage Kakbhushundi predicts:

> *In the Kali Yuga, a time of great sin, men and women are steeped in unrighteousness and go against the teachings of the Vedas. Virtue is overwhelmed by the sins of this age; all good literature has vanished; and false leaders have created their own beliefs. People are caught in delusion, and all acts of devotion have been consumed by greed.*

1.8.6. Concept of Dharma (धर्म)

Dharma can be described as a path of righteousness. By fulfilling one's Dharma, individuals accumulate good merits or Karmas, which contribute to the goal of attaining Moksha. Key aspects of Dharma include patience, forgiveness, self-control, honesty, purity of thought, mastery of the senses, truthfulness, reasoning, anger management, non-violence, knowledge, and continuous learning. For example, practicing patience when faced with challenges or demonstrating forgiveness toward someone who has wronged you are both essential elements of Dharma.

---

[45] Dr. Vineet Aggarwal, Mumbai. India.

Right View

Right Mindfulness

Right Intention

Right Concentration

Right Speech

Right Effort

Right Action

Right Livelihood

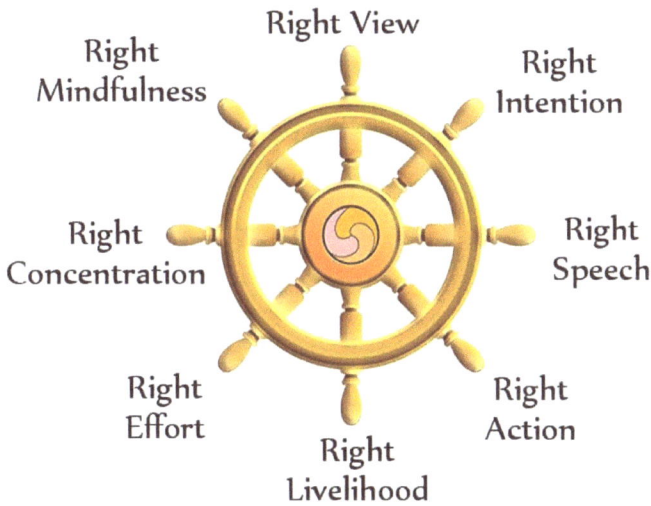

Figure 30 - Dharma Wheel

Dharma is a fundamental principle of Hinduism, a religion with over a billion followers. Hindus believe that Dharma was revealed in the Vedas. The term derives from the Sanskrit word "dhri," which means to uphold or sustain and can be translated as "religion," "law," "order," "duty," or "ethics." It encompasses all the principles, purposes, influences, and institutions that shape a person's character, both individually and socially. It serves as the law of right living, ensuring happiness on earth and spiritual salvation. For instance, observing ethical practices in business or honouring family commitments reflects one's commitment to Dharma.

Defining Dharma can be challenging, but it is often described as those which uplift living beings. Anything that promotes the welfare of others is considered Dharma. The wise rishis have declared that what sustains life is Dharma.

Dharma encompasses every form of righteous conduct essential for individual and societal welfare. Those who adhere to the principles of Dharma naturally attain Moksha (eternal bliss). Thus, Dharma, Artha (prosperity), Kama (desire), and Moksha shape the four goals of life.

Ritual actions are also integral to Dharma. Properly performing rituals is crucial for organizing both individual lives and communities. The Dharmashastras, which are the earliest sources of Hindu law, detail various rituals. For example, it is part of Dharma to name and bless a child, to initiate their education, and to perform the last rites for parents. These rituals play a significant role in maintaining the order of the world. Failing to act according to one's own Dharma is deemed wrong and referred to as adharma. In the Bhagavad Gita, Krishna states that whenever adharma overshadows Dharma, he will manifest on earth to protect the righteous and eliminate the wicked.

Individuals have different obligations and duties based on their age, gender, and social position. While Dharma is universal, it also varies according to specific circumstances, meaning that each person has their own unique Dharma.

Dharma also represents the social order, defining one's duty within the divisions of society known as varna (caste) or Jati (birth group). The Rigveda identifies four varnas, which are derived from different parts of the body of the divine being that created the universe: Brahmins (priests), Kshatriyas (warriors), Vaisyas (merchants), and Sudras (servants). Each varna serves God's creation in its way; for instance, priests fulfill their roles through spirituality, warriors through heroism, merchants through their skills, and servants through their service. When each varna performs its respective duties, society is considered just and aligned with Dharma. Acting by Dharma is seen as a service to both humanity and God[46].

✓ *The Bhagavad Gita Chapter in my upcoming book is entirely dedicated to explaining the concepts of Dharma and Karma.*

---

[46] Agarwal, R. "Dharma/Dhamma". In Athyal.J.M (ed). *Religions in Southeast Asia: An Encyclopedia of Faiths and Cultures*. ABC-CLIO, 2015.

1.8.7. Concept of Karma (कर्म)

The term "Karma" is inherently complex, so I aim to present a concise and simplified overview of the topic, so it is easy to understand by viewers.

What is "Karma"?

Figure 31 - Karma Illustrated

The Law of Karma represents the principle of Action and Reaction. This law states that every action we take is recorded and rewarded based on the good or evil it brings about. It is a universal law that applies to everyone; no one can escape its reach or manipulate its effects. Even actions done in secret, away from the public eye, are captured by the Law of Karma. The term "Karma" literally means

"ACTION," but its widespread recognition has expanded its meaning to signify a cosmic principle.

Why is this law relevant?

Consider a scenario where something unexpected and unfortunate occurs without any apparent reason. In such instances, we might remark, "Karma!" acknowledging that this event is a manifestation of the Law of Karma at work, as it reflects a reaction to a past action—one that may be long forgotten. The Law of Karma ensures that every action is appropriately addressed.

An Example of Karma

Imagine a garden filled with apple trees. How did these apples come to be? It wasn't magic or random chance; someone had to plant apple seeds for those trees to grow. Perhaps it was you, neighbours, or maybe even birds that scattered the seeds. The apples are the outcome of a deliberate action—planting seeds. This reflects a fundamental truth: to harvest apples, you first need to plant apple seeds; planting tomatoes won't produce mangoes. Though this principle may not be directly provable, we grasp it through observation and inference.

For instance, you can't directly prove the Law of Gravity exists. You can't show ownership of it as you would with a personal account by revealing a password. However, if you toss your phone into the air and it falls back to the ground, you can infer that a force is acting upon it—this is how we come to accept the Law of Gravity as a fact. Similarly, Karma can also be verified through the results we observe in our lives.

The Complexity of Karma

The Law of Karma is multifaceted. Sometimes you may receive the consequences of your actions immediately; other times, it may take days, months, or even years for the effects to manifest. Hinduism believes that this law remains in effect even after death.

Consider the idea of Cause and Effect: for every effect, there must be a cause. What occurs now is the result of something that happened in the past. For instance, if you see smoke, there must be a fire or another source of that smoke. This principle is evident in our daily experiences. Think about a pot, a plate, and a statue; they are all made from mud. The mud is the cause, while the items are its effects. Thus, the events happening around us are the consequences of our past actions or Karma, which the Law of Karma recognizes. Therefore, Karma is often referred to as both "the Law of Action and Reaction" and "the Law of Cause and Effect."

The Law of Karma is straightforward: "What you give is what you get." Though simple enough for a child to understand, we often overlook this truth, forgetting Karma's impact on our lives. Just as the Law of Gravity keeps everything grounded, whether we think about it or not, the Law of Karma is a universal force that affects everyone equally, no matter who they are.

The irony is that, like action itself, no one can escape the effects of Karma. We all take action daily—getting up, moving forward, and making choices—and every action brings a reaction. This is the essence of Karma, known across cultures and religions as the Law of Cause and Effect. It means that the outcomes in our lives reflect our past actions, for good or for ill.

The Law of Karma governs not only our present lives but also our existence beyond this one. By understanding the three aspects of Karma, we can see that our current circumstances are the outcomes of our past actions, as dictated by this law. Nothing in our lives is purely coincidental; every event we experience is a manifestation of our Karma returning to us. Each of our actions is noted by the law, categorized as good or bad, kind or cruel, and positive or negative. The law employs its means to assess our actions and document our Karma. Every misdeed is logged by the Law of Karma, and there is no escaping its consequences. Eventually, it will all return to us in one form or another. This is the essence of how the Law of Karma operates.

Karmic Cycle

Though "Karma" translates to action, it doesn't solely mean physical deeds. Instead, karma encompasses action on three levels: body, mind, and energy. Every action on these levels leaves a subtle imprint within you. It's straightforward to grasp – your senses constantly gather information from the outside world, which accumulates over time into distinct patterns. These patterns gradually shape behavioral tendencies, eventually solidifying into what you recognize as your personality, or what you believe to be your true nature. The process also works in reverse; your mind influences how you perceive the world, forming your karma – a self-created orientation to life, often shaped in unconsciousness. What you think of as "me" is largely an accumulation of habits and tendencies you've developed over time, without awareness of how they formed[47].

Figure 32 - The Karmic Cycle

Karmic cycles are recurring patterns in life that often reflect past hurts or mistakes. Spiritually, these cycles aim to offer valuable lessons and guide you through healing from past trauma. For example, if you repeatedly find yourself in relationships that feel unbalanced, it might point to an unresolved pattern. Breaking free from a karmic cycle involves practicing self-forgiveness, being mindful, and releasing any lingering resentment toward others.

Karmic Connection

A karmic connection is someone you encounter repeatedly throughout your life, and it's not by chance. Each meeting is intended to offer mutual learning—this person is meant to teach you something about yourself, and you, in turn, are meant to teach them. Often, when

---

[47] Karma. Yogi's guide to crafting your destiny by Sadhguru.

we first meet a karmic connection, it's because they hold a lesson that's essential for our personal growth. Whether they are a central figure or a passing acquaintance, we feel drawn to them because they can help us advance spiritually. In a sense, they act as a spiritual guide on our journey, keeping us aligned with our higher self or sole purpose. This type of relationship can be between people of the same genders or opposite ones.

There are two types of karmic relationships:

Figure 33 - Karmic Relationship

- Karmic Relationships from Previous Lives

  This type of relationship describes a connection between two people believed to stem from unresolved issues or unfinished business from past lives. Rooted in the spiritual idea of karma, it suggests that actions and choices made in previous lives influence relationships in this one.

  For example, someone might feel an intense bond with a person they've just met, sensing familiarity or a sense of "unfinished business." This could be viewed as a karmic relationship, where past-life connections or unresolved matters have carried over into the present.

- Karmic Relationship created by you in this life.

  This type of relationship describes a connection or a bond between two individuals that they build in their current life. They can be as fulfilling and monumental as long-term partnerships.

Relationship with Rebirth

Given that every thought, intention, and action carry consequences, karmic connections are intricately linked to the law of karma. When spirits form significant relationships, they often generate karma, which can be either positive or negative depending on their interactions. Acts of compassion, love, or support foster positive karma, while conflict, harm, or unresolved emotional issues can lead to negative karmic ties. Karma is also intertwined with the concept of reincarnation, creating a continuous cycle of birth and death influenced by karma, which connects individuals to their past and future lives. In the process of reincarnation, the spirit or soul persists after death and is reborn into a new form, whether human or nonhuman. The nature of rebirth—whether as an animal, human, or insect—depends on the resolution of negative karma and the cultivation of positive karma.

Karmic accounts do not cease with death; they persist across lifetimes. Although the body dies, the soul is reborn carrying its karma. This cycle indicates that death is not the end but merely a transition. Our karma propels us into new lives repeatedly until we attain moksha. As long as karma exists, rebirth occurs, and while we are alive, we continue to create karma[48].

Karma is thought to initiate a cycle of birth, death, and rebirth known as samsara. This cycle persists until we manage to break free from the grip of karma and achieve liberation or enlightenment. Each lifetime

---

[48] Karma. Indian Philosophy & Its Impact on Life. Britannica. Accessed 9/5/2023.

offers us chances to learn and grow from the results of our actions, ultimately guiding us toward spiritual evolution.

※

The Bhagavad Gita teachings will be discussed in more depth in my upcoming book on Scriptures.

2. APPENDIXES

2.1. Table of Figures

Figure 1 - Symbols used in Hinduism...17

Figure 2 – The Greater Indus Valley 1900 BCE 24

Figure 3 - Vedic Period Teachings...26

Figure 4 - Hinduism Scriptures...33

Figure 5 – Pictorial representation of the Medieval Period................37

Figure 6 - Map of India in 1525 38

Figure 7 - The Bhakti Movement in Hinduism 39

Figure 8 - Map of Medieval Period of India.....................................41

Figure 9 - Pre-Modern Period. King Akhbar 51

Figure 10 - British Period...53

Figure 11 - Post Indian Independence Period 57

Figure 12 - Symbol of Religions 59

Figure 13 - Lord Shiva in Meditation..63

Figure 14 - Lord Vishnu in Celestial Splendor 64

Figure 15 - Shaktism Goddess 66

Figure 16 - Lord Ganesha 67

Figure 17 - Lord Surya..67

Figure 18 - Sringeri Temple, Sringeri, Karnataka. India. 68

Figure 19 - Caste System in Hinduism 72

Figure 20 - Representation of Moksha..80

Figure 21 - Atman - The Soul...81

Figure 22 - Samsara Illustrated 83

Figure 23 - Picture Illustrating Good Karma.....................................84

Figure 24 – Rishi holding Hinduism Scripture 85

Figure 25 - Cyclical Time Illustrated...86

Figure 26 - Satya-Yug Period..88

Figure 27 - Treta Yug Period 90

Figure 28 - Dvapara Yuga Period...91

Figure 29 - Kali Yug Period: Yug of Destruction.............................93

Figure 30 - Dharma Wheel...95

Figure 31 - Karma Illustrated 97

Figure 32 - The Karmic Cycle 100

Figure 33 - Karmic Relationship 101

2.2. English Glossary

GLOSSARY

Adharma - Adharma (अधर्म) is a Sanskrit term that means "unrighteousness, injustice, or disorder." It is the opposite of Dharma, which represents righteousness, moral duty, and truth.. 96

Advaita - Advaita (अद्वैत) means "non-duality" and is a school of Hindu philosophy that teaches that the individual self (Atman) and the ultimate reality (Brahman) are one and the same. It is a core concept in Advaita Vedanta, a system of thought developed by Adi Shankaracharya (8th century CE)... 44, 45, 63, 68

Asuras - Asuras (असुर) are powerful beings often described as demons, anti-gods, or titans who oppose the Devas (gods)... 32

Chaturvarna - The Chaturvarna system (चार वर्ण) is the traditional Hindu social classification mentioned in the Vedas... 73

Din-i-Ilahi - Religious doctrine introduced by Mughal Emperor Akbar in 1582 CE as an attempt to blend elements of Hinduism, Islam, Jainism, Christianity, and Zoroastrianism into a universal faith. The name Din-i-Ilahi means "Religion of God.".. 52

Dravidians - Dravidians are an ethnic and linguistic group primarily found in South India, Sri Lanka, and parts of Pakistan, Nepal, and Bangladesh. They are believed to be among the earliest inhabitants of the Indian subcontinent, with a rich cultural and historical heritage... 35

Henotheism - Henotheism is the belief in and worship of one primary deity while acknowledging the existence of other gods. It differs from monotheism (which recognizes only one God) and polytheism (which worships multiple gods equally)... 61

Hermits - A hermit is a person who chooses to live in solitude, away from society, often for spiritual, religious, or philosophical reasons. In Hinduism, hermits are known as sages (rishis), ascetics (sannyasis), or renunciants (yogis) who withdraw from worldly life to focus on meditation, self-discipline, and seeking higher truth.. 29

Hindutva - Hindutva (हिन्दुत्व) is a term that means "Hinduness" and refers to the cultural, historical, and national identity associated with Hindu civilization. It was popularized by Vinayak Damodar Savarkar in 1923 in his book Hindutva: Who is a Hindu?... .... 55, 56, 59

Hymns - A hymn is a sacred song or poem that is used in religious worship or spiritual expression. In the context of Hinduism and the Rig Veda, hymns (suktas) are verses composed in praise of deities, cosmic forces, and philosophical ideas.. 27, 28, 29, 30

Monasteries - A monastery is a spiritual and religious institution where monks, nuns, or ascetics live in seclusion to dedicate their lives to prayer, meditation, and spiritual discipline.. 49, 68

Sahasrara - Sahasrara (सहस्रार) is the seventh and highest chakra in the Kundalini yoga system, often referred to as the Crown Chakra. The word Sahasrara means "thousand-petaled" in Sanskrit, symbolizing infinite consciousness and spiritual enlightenment.. 66

Sati - Sati (सती) was an ancient Hindu practice where a widow self-immolated on her husband's funeral pyre. It was considered an act of supreme devotion and purity, but over time, it became a forced or expected ritual in some communities, leading to social and ethical concerns............................ 47

Shaivism - Shaivism (शैव सम्प्रदाय) is one of the major traditions of Hinduism that worships Lord Shiva as the Supreme God. It is an ancient sect with deep spiritual, philosophical, and devotional roots... ....40, 45, 61, 62, 65

Vaishnava - Vaishnavism (वैष्णव सम्प्रदाय) is a major tradition of Hinduism that worships Lord Vishnu as the Supreme God. Followers of this tradition, known as Vaishnavas, believe that Vishnu and his avatars (such as Rama and Krishna) are the ultimate divine beings responsible for the creation, preservation, and protection of the universe... ....40, 45, 64, 70

Vedanta - Vedanta (वेदान्त) is a philosophical school of Hinduism that explores the nature of reality, the self (Atman), and the ultimate truth (Brahman). The word Vedanta means "the end of the Vedas", referring to teachings found in the Upanishads, which form the final part of the Vedic scriptures... .... 33, 44, 45, 52, 68

Vedas: The Vedas are a collection of ancient Indian texts that form the oldest and most authoritative scriptures of Hinduism. Composed in Sanskrit, the

Vedas are primarily religious hymns, prayers, and rituals, used in the worship of deities and to guide religious and social practices.7, 16, 17, 18, 20, 21, 28, 31, 32, 33, 36, 37, 40, 55, 62, 63, 65, 66, 68, 70, 72, 73, 79, 86, 94, 95

Vidur - Vidur (विदुर) was a wise statesman, philosopher, and advisor in the Mahabharata, known for his intelligence, righteousness, and deep understanding of Dharma (duty and morality)... 58

End of Book

Read my Upcoming Books,

Shastra Wisdom

Consecrated Scriptures of Hinduism

Books Available on Amazon Worldwide

www.ingramcontent.com/pod-product-compliance
Lightning Source LLC
Chambersburg PA
CBHW041958090426
42811CB00025B/1926/J